Revelation as Drama

REVELATION AS DRAMA

James L. Blevins

BROADMAN PRESS
Nashville, Tennessee

4213-93
ISBN: 0-8054-1393-6

Dewey Decimal Classification: 228
Subject Heading: BIBLE. N.T. REVELATION
Library of Congress Catalog Card Number: 84-4986
Printed in the United States of America

The Bible texts in this publication are from the Revised Standard Version of the Bible, copyrighted 1946, 1952, © 1971, 1973 by the National Council of Churches of Christ in the U.S.A., and used by permission.

Library of Congress Cataloging in Publication Data

Blevins, James L.
  Revelation as drama.

  1. Bible. N.T. Revelation—Criticism, interpretation,
etc. I. Title.
BS2825.2.B57   1984   228'.06   84-4986
ISBN 0-8054-1393-6 (pbk.)

This book is dedicated to the laypersons
who labor for Christ in the local churches
like my mother
Lona Marie Blevins
(1912-1983)

The drama script is dedicated to all of the hundreds of students at The Southern Baptist Theological Seminary who have participated with me in dramatizing the Book of Revelation. These students have helped me to write and refine the script, and given excellent suggestions concerning the staging of Revelation on the ancient stage at Ephesus. It is my hope and prayer that one day we will be able to go to Ephesus and do the performance of Revelation there and film it for use in our local churches.

Contents

Illustrations

Introduction to Revelation

John's Testimony

Greetings! I am John, one of the twelve disciples, and author of the Book of Revelation. I would like to share with you my personal testimony of the time in which I wrote, of the burden that God placed upon my heart. I came to Ephesus after the death of Jesus on the cross and became the spiritual leader of the churches in that area. I served a long ministry in the area of Asia Minor and was well into my nineties when the great catastrophe happened in the Roman Empire. Caesar Domitian came into power in AD 81 and declared that he was a divine being. He sent out orders across the empire, instructing local communities to erect a statue of himself so that all the inhabitants could be called upon to worship at this statue and to pronounce Caesar as Lord. I still remember that day in Ephesus as I was walking through the city square and read the proclamation that had been posted. Shortly, a huge statue of Caesar Domitian was erected in the main square of Ephesus, a statue some sixteen feet tall. It was hollow on the inside so that the local priests could go in and make it talk and perform all kinds of wonders.

I realized that this would pose grave difficulties for the Christians in Asia Minor, for we as believers recognized only one Lord, Jesus Christ. I encouraged the Christians to resist the worship of Caesar Domitian's statue. Many Christians were persecuted and some were put to death. In the church at Pergamum, a young man named Antipas was arrested and boiled alive in hot oil in the city square because of his testimony to Christ. I, myself, was arrested and sent some 60 miles off the coast of Ephesus to the prison island of Patmos. There I was forced to quarry rock in the hot sunshine.

In the cool of the evening we prisoners would be led up the hillside and locked into a cave. Many evenings I stood at the entrance to the cave, looking out at the blue Aegean Sea, as still as a sea of glass.

11

One evening as I stood looking out of the mouth of the cave, I heard a voice behind me saying, "John, John, write down the things that I will reveal to you." Over a period of nine months I received these revelations and wrote them in a scroll to be sent to the persecuted Christians in Asia Minor.

Because I was in a Roman prison I could not openly speak of Christ, so the Spirit led me to write the revelation of Jesus Christ in the apocalyptic codes of the Jewish people. Some 200 or 300 years before the birth of Christ, the Jewish people had developed a coded language so that they could speak to one another about their relationship to God. Throughout their history the Jewish people had been a persecuted people, who desperately needed such a code. I wrote Revelation in these same codes, because mine was a prison experience and the Christians on the mainland were facing persecution. I would like to share these codes with you, my dear readers, in order that you might be prepared to understand the Book of Revelation. The very first word in Revelation in the Greek text is the word, *apocalypsis*. It has as its basic meaning to decode, uncover, or reveal. Thus, in your modern Bibles, my book is called the Revelation. That word is used to give you the clue that Revelation belongs to a special kind of literature and is written in this coded language in the tradition of my Jewish people.

In your modern world I understand that under Idi Amin in Uganda the Christians developed a special, coded language, so that they might speak to one another about their Christian experience. This has been the case throughout Christian history. If you have traveled through the catacombs in Rome, you have also seen the symbols and codes of the early Christians inscribed on the walls. For example, the fish is a representation for Christianity.

Let me now share with you the codes for the Book of Revelation. They are threefold. First, the number code is presented, with every number in Revelation having a symbolic meaning.

Number Code

TWELVE: Wholeness, especially in reference to people. (Thus the number of 144,000 in Rev. 7 is based upon 12 and implies the whole people of God.)

TEN: Complete number. (Thus, the thousand year reign of Christ in ch. 20 implies a complete reign of Christ.)

SEVEN: Divine number. (In many apocalyptic works the code number for God is 777; many Jews added up the number of their name according to the Hebrew alphabet and this would be their code number in days of persecution. Revelation makes great use of 7s; seven trumpets, seven churches, seven bowls of wrath.)

SIX: Imperfection or extreme evil. (In Revelation, 666 is the code number for Caesar Domitian, who had persecuted and put Christians to death.)

FIVE: Penalty. (All major punishments and penalities are given in series of 5s, the locusts that come up out of the pit torture people for five months.)

FOUR: World. (Angels stand at the four corners of the earth.)

TWO: Witnessing. (Two witnesses appear in Revelation 11.)

ONE: Unity.

FRACTIONS: Incompleteness. (Found in Act III, showing one third of things being destroyed and standing for incompleteness.)

The second code which I use in my book is the color code. Colors carry symbolic meanings.

Color Code

PALE GREEN: Death. (The fourth horse in my book is a pale green horse and Hades follows behind.)

DARK GREEN: Life. (Around the throne of God in chapter 4 is a dark green, emerald rainbow symbolizing life.)

WHITE: Purity or conquering.

RED: Warfare.

BLACK: Famine. (In ch. 6 four horsemen appear, the white horse of conquering, followed by the red horse of warfare, then the black horse of famine, and last the pale green horse of death.)

GOLD: Worth or value.

BRONZE: Strength.

SCARLET: Sin.

In chapter 1 of my book I describe the Son of Man in color codes. I was in prison for preaching Christ, I could not openly speak about him, so I set forth a living sermon in colors. The Son of Man is described with bronze feet, depicting strength, white robes of conquering, white hair of purity, gold band around his chest, representing his worth or value, a sharp, two-edged sword coming from his mouth, standing for piercing words. All the Christians hearing this passage read aloud would have known immediately the one of whom I am speaking.

The third code in Revelation is the animal code.

Animal Code

FROG: The meanest, vilest animal in my world was considered to be the frog; anytime the frog appears, evil is right behind it. In Revelation 16:13, *three* frogs appear and then the last battle between good and evil. Watch out for the frog!

EAGLE: Next to the frog, the eagle always brings bad news. In the midst of the seven trumpets, the eagle appears to announce that the last trumpets will be far worse than the first trumpets. Even when the eagle is not present, I use the cry of the eagle, *ouai*, translated in your Bible as *woe*. The English translation, however, does not capture the original sound of the Greek word which, if pronounced quickly, sounds like the screech of an eagle. Thus, the last trumpets in Revelation are called the first *ouai*, second *ouai*, and third *ouai*. In chapter 18 of Revelation the businessmen of the earth, the ship captains, and the kings come on stage and sing three *ouai* songs.

MONSTER BEASTS: Many of you have been concerned about the monster beasts in my book. Please bear in mind that monster beasts represent monstrous persons or forces. They are constructed from bits and parts of wild animals to represent extremely evil persons.

BEAST FROM THE SEA: A symbol for Caesar Domitian or political power. It is composed of the three symbols of the major world powers in my day: bear's feet—Medea, leopard's spots—Persia, lion's head—Rome. There was no animal mean enough to represent Caesar, who had put to death so many Christians.

SEA SERPENT: Satan is depicted by this monster beast, a red sea serpent with seven heads. My Jewish people feared the ocean and the sea serpents in it, so what could be better to depict Satan than this horrible creature from the sea?

LOCUSTS: Monster locusts came up out of the bottomless pit. They have men's faces, women's hair, scorpion tails, and are the size of horses. They represent the sin and decay of the Roman Empire or any society that opposes God.

SEVEN-HORNED LAMB: Jesus, himself, is depicted by an animal, a lamb with seven horns (divine power) and seven eyes (divine seeing).

Because I was in prison I could not openly speak of Christ, so I used this coded animal to symbolize my Lord.

LION: Often symbolizes all wild creatures.

Ox: Often symbolizes all domesticated creatures.

Every animal has a meaning. Take three different color pens and underline each of the three codes as you read through my Book of Revelation. The Roman people did not have these codes and did not understand them. Because of this, I was able to send Revelation from my prison island to the mainland, where my book was read aloud in the churches to give them comfort and hope in their days of persecution. Roman soldiers probably thought the sun had just been too hot on this old man's head.

Finally, I would like to say to you modern readers that I saw these things; these are visionary experiences. I heard the beautiful music found in my book. I could not express what I had experienced in prose. Instead, I chose this dramatic medium to express that which I had beheld. You cannot come to Revelation and just read it on the printed page. You must use all of your senses; you must see it, hear it, read it, open yourselves up to its great majesty. I selected the dramatic medium to capture some of the excitement of my experience and share it with my people. In Ephesus was the largest amphitheater of the Roman world, holding 25,000 people. In it were performed the great Greek tragic dramas. Tragic drama was always religious drama; a throne to God was always on the main stage; a chorus of 12 or 24 stood around the throne and sang the music of the drama; the actors were called priests. At the end of the drama, God was always brought down from the upper level of the stage to solve the dilemmas posed in the drama. This huge amphitheater stood at the major junction of the street in Ephesus. Sailing toward the harbor of Ephesus you could see this theater a mile out to sea, its gleaming white seats shining in the sun. Anywhere you went in Ephesus you were confronted by this huge theater. It is even mentioned in the Book of Acts. I lived in Ephesus over 50 years and this theater was imprinted upon my mind.

A most unusual thing about the theater is that it was made up of a series of seven windows for the depiction of stage scenery. There was a lower level or orchestra level for the choir standing around the throne of God; next was a ledge for one main actor to stand upon; finally, seven windows display the scenery. It was the only theater in the ancient world with seven windows; all others have three or five such windows. Thus, the number seven was an important number for producing drama in the theater in Ephesus. As many have recognized, seven is the key number in my own Book of Revelation, dividing it into seven acts with seven scenes.

Many of the Christians who had joined the church of Asia Minor had come out of a background where their religious experiences were expressed in drama. In the mystery religions drama played a very significant role. The Temple cult of the Old Testament made use of the dramatic; in the early Christian worship, drama was also very much a part. Thus, I used this medium to express my own experiences and revelations from God. The directions which are given in my book can actually be used to stage the drama in the theater at Ephesus, especially with its seven windows. In my day I had no actual hope that the book would ever be presented in Ephesus, because of the persecution of the Christians. However, I wanted to use the dramatic medium so that when the book was read aloud in the worship services, the dramatic overtones could be perceived by the listeners. This sevenfold pattern that the people were so accustomed to would help the book come alive for them.

I wish you well as you begin your journey through my book and I pray that its dramatic power will be unveiled in your life. The first blessing in my book is found in chapter 1, verse 3, "Blessed is he who reads aloud these words." One of the most important things you can do as you read Revelation is to read it aloud and experience its exciting impact.

Thank you, John, for your testimony and the great help that you have given us in understanding the codes in which you wrote your book. This testimony of John helps us to see that Revelation belongs to a distinct kind of literature, apocalyptic literature, in which much emphasis was placed on symbols and codes. Revelation is the only representative of this kind of literature in the New Testament.

The Ephesian Theater and Revelation

Many scholars have viewed Revelation as drama in its form; many others have spoken of the dramatic qualities in the last book of the

Bible. However, up to this time no one has attempted to place the book in the setting of the theater at Ephesus. From John's testimony we have learned that he sought to express the dramatic qualities of his own vision in the literary device of Greek tragic drama. It is very important that we see the significance of the theater at Ephesus for his dramatic expression. This great theater is mentioned in the Book of Acts (19:29). There some of Paul's friends were brought into the theater during a riot occasioned by the silversmiths. For many hours the crowd chanted, "Great is Artemis of the Ephesians" (v. 28). The theater was located in the very heart of the city, at the intersection of the city's two principal streets. The theater was built on the slopes of the mountain at Ephesus in the third century BC. For over 300 years, the great Greek tragedies and comedies had been enacted upon its stage. Historians of Greek drama are puzzled by one unique aspect of the stage building of the theater. To understand that uniqueness, we must first look at the basic parts of a Greek theater, using the Ephesian stage as our model.

On the lower level was a circular orchestra. Directly behind the orchestra lay the *skene* or scene building. In its earliest days, third century BC, it had been a wooden structure. By the first century AD it had become a permanent stone edifice. The *proskene* jutted out from the stage building, to form a raised platform or stage, 8 1/2 feet above the orchestra level and 10 feet deep. The upper portion of the *skene* was called the *episkene* and usually contained 3 to 5 openings for scenery in Greek drama. These openings were called *thuromata*. Pillars 1 1/2 feet wide separated these *thuromata*.

The stage at Ephesus is the only such stage building ever excavated with seven thuromata or windows. Thus, for nearly 300 years before the writing of Revelation, the number of seven had acquired great significance for the inhabitants of Ephesus. The main purpose of these windows was to effect presentation of scenery in Greek drama. Painted panels were placed in the windows, depicting scenes too difficult to perform on the stage. This suits well many of the scenes in Revelation.

In addition, a revolving-door structure called an *eccyclema* could be placed in the windows and be turned to show three additional scenes. At times, this revolving-door structure would be rolled out on the main platform, adding another dimension to the drama. The seven windows of the Ephesian stage had a great bearing on the way

THE EPHESIAN THEATER

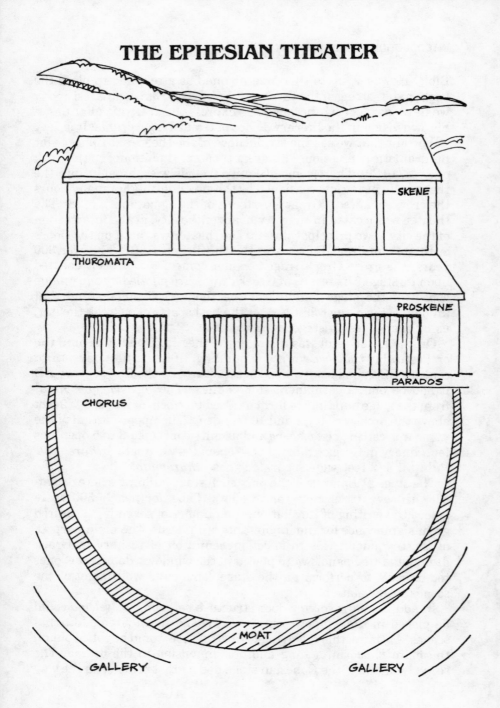

the dramas were presented there. They also seem to have had the same effect on the organization of Revelation.

Above the windows was the very top of the scene building. This area was always reserved for the abode of the gods. A machine, a type of crane, would transport messengers from the gods down to the *proskene* level. In many of the extant Greek tragedies, the final solution of the drama is brought by a god coming down to solve the dilemma.

The Chorus

The role of the chorus in Greek tragedy and comedy has been neglected, along with the significance of the stage at Ephesus. The chorus composed of either 12 or 24 men entered the theater on either side of the *skene* through the *parados*. The chorus represented the objective intention of the author and offered comments on the events on stage. The chorus could represent for instance, wasps, birds, frogs, goats, snakes, bees, fish, or storks. These representations would be carried out by assuming masks. In most of the Greek tragedies the chorus was friendly to the main character. The chorus was the most important aspect of the Greek tragedy, interpreting in musical phrases and songs the action of the play for the audience. They were usually positioned in a semicircle around the throne of Dionysius, directly in front of the permanent altar, located on the orchestra level. In fact, the earliest tragedies had only chorus, no actors.

Choruses could also be divided into groups of 2 or 4 with the leader appointed for each group. The chorus could sing and chant, accompanied by lyres or harps which they carried. They chanted measured antiphonous strains, balanced strophe and antistrophe. In Revelation the 24 elders serve as the chorus. They stand around the throne of God in chapters 4 and 5 and sing five beautiful hymns. They also could have donned face masks to represent various beasts or animals presented in Revelation. They sing some 30 hymns scattered throughout the book. The great composer Handel was so inspired by the hymns of Revelation that he made them a very vital part of his work, the *Messiah*. Careful study of these thirty hymns indicates that the chorus served the same role in Revelation as it did in Greek tragedy, interpreting the action on the stage. In many places these elders lead John around heaven and interpret what he beholds.

In Act I of Revelation the chorus responds to each of the seven letters with the music, "Hear what the Spirit says to the churches." In Act II there is a chorus of four living creatures singing, "Holy, Holy, Holy" in God's throne room, followed by the 24 elders singing, "Blessing to the Lamb." In chapters 4 and 5 there are five hymns, each one expanding, first the four living creatures, joined by the 24 elders, then the thousands of angels. Finally, the fifth hymn is sung by the inhabitants of heaven, earth, and those under the earth. Each of the seven acts of Revelation has some musical presentation by the choir of 24 elders; they remain on the orchestra level throughout the drama.

The Form of Greek Tragedy

A typical tragedy was divided into definite parts. These plays began with a prologue which was done in the form of a monologue or dialogue. One character acquainted the audience with the necessary background information for the play. This type of prologue is found in Revelation 1:1-8. John represents in monologue form the background information for the drama. After the prologue the chorus entered the stage by way of the *parados,* usually singing. They do so in Revelation, singing the hymn passages of 1:6-8, punctuated with the dual amen. They remained on the stage of the drama to comment on and interpret the following events.

After the entrance of the chorus the first episode took place. It was composed of dialogue of no more than three actors or a monologue followed by a stasimon or choral ode. Its basic pattern, episode-stasimon, is repeated 3, 5, or 7 times. Revelation fits the sevenfold pattern and the stage at Ephesus itself.

Following the last episode, the exodus of the choir or chorus took place and then the epilogue. A survey of Greek tragedies indicates that some were basic plays of one actor with the chorus filling in with responses and a variety of other roles. A monologue with choral response might very well have made a Greek tragedy. Revelation falls into that pattern. In the Greek tragedy, *The Suppliants,* the chorus sang 565 verses out of a total of 1,674. The chorus leader, in addition, spoke 90 verses. Instead of acts the Greeks used the word *part,* which denoted merely a division of the play as determined by choral division of the written or interpolated action. Revelation can be divided into seven such parts or acts.

The Stage Setting

Let us now attempt to determine how the stage settings of Revelation are related to the specific situation of the seven window stage at Ephesus. The text of Revelation contains instructions for these stage settings.

For Act I, The Seven Golden Lampstands, the stage setting is found in 1:9-20. The stage building represents the Temple with the focus on the holy place. In fact, in each act of Revelation, some aspect of the Temple will be featured. In verses 12-20 John describes the stage setting, the seven golden lampstands with the Son of Man standing in their midst. The lampstand represents a church in each of the seven windows (quite likely the seven-branch menorah). As each window opens, the message is read to the church. After each letter, the choir, located in the orchestra level, responds with, "He who has an ear let him hear what the Spirit says to the churches."

Act II, The Seven Seal Visions, in chapters 4 and 5 shows the stage setting of the throne room of God. The theme from the Temple is the altar of sacrifice as it stands on center stage. God's throne room is described in minute detail, a throne surrounded by four living creatures and 24 elders, with seven burning torches in front of the throne. A sea of glass separates earth from heaven. God has a scroll with seven seals upon it. A lamb appears on stage to take the scroll. As the seven seals are opened, we see the seven seal visions in the seven windows of the stage building.

For Act III, The Seven Trumpets, the stage setting is found in 8:5-6. The theme from the Temple is the altar of incense; it is featured on the back of the stage. Seven angels come out of the Temple on the ledge of the stage and station themselves in front of the seven windows of the stage building. As each angel walks to the ledge of the stage to blow his trumpet, a picture of the destruction of the plague which is announced appears in the window.

In Act IV, The Seven Tableaux, the background shows the holy of holies open and the ark of the covenant, the symbol of God's faithfulness, in the midst of the struggle of good and evil. Seven different scenes of the struggle are presented in seven windows. The choir interprets the action with a hymn, 12:10b-12. The concluding ode is in 15:3b-4.

For Act V, The Seven Bowls of Wrath visions, the stage setting is found in 15:5-8 and 16:1. The curtains to the holy of holies are closed and smoke comes forth, emphasizing the judgment of God now before us. Seven angels come out on the ledge of the stage and position themselves once again in front of the seven windows of the stage building. As each walks to the edge of the ledge to pour out his bowl, a painting of the ensuing plague appears on the window behind the angel.

In Act VI, The Seven Judgments, the stage setting is found in 17:1-3a. The whole stage building becomes the Temple. In front of the Temple we see Rome burning. A scarlet beast appears, symbolizing Rome. The seven last judgments are depicted in the seven windows of the stage building.

For Act VII, The Seven Great Promises, visions of victory, the stage setting is found in 19:11 to 20:4a. Heaven is open and the Temple now descends to earth. The Lamb is the Temple. We see seven great promises of victory that will belong to the Christians. The millenial reign of Christ takes place and the new Jerusalem is depicted in the windows of the stage building.

The Prologue

The drama of Revelation begins with the prologue (1:1-8). The choir makes its entrance through the *parados,* prepares to sing, stationing itself around the throne of God on the lower orchestra level of the stage at Ephesus. John, the only actor in the drama, appears on the ledge of the stage building. The drama begins, then, with a monologue on the past of John, interspersed with choral odes from the choir.

In this monologue John sets forth that the Revelation had been given to him directly by God. He also speaks of his own imprisonment on the Isle of Patmos due to his testimony for Jesus Christ. Patmos was used by the Romans as a prison island; the church fathers tell us that this island was used to quarry rock and was a very barren place. In fact, there was no natural water supply on the island; all the water had to be brought in by ship.

John makes much of the theme of being a witness even unto death throughout his Book of Revelation. The word *witness* comes from the word *martus* from which we get our word *martyr.* Thus, at the very beginning of the book John emphasizes his own witness, even to the point of death.

In 1:3 we encounter the first blessing in the book. It is directed to those who read and hear the words of the prophecy. The Book of Revelation would have been read aloud in the churches as it was received. Reading aloud would have captured much of the dramatic overtone of the book. However, very early the church attempted to dramatize parts of the book in addition to reading it aloud. In the first communion services, seven candlesticks would be lighted and the letters would be read to the churches, as the church broke bread and shared the cup.

In 1:4 John addresses the letter to seven churches in Asia Minor with the typical words of greeting found in so many letters of the New Testament. The seven churches are selected from about fifteen in Asia Minor. Seven is the divine number. In addition, if one locates the seven churches on the map of Asia Minor and draws connecting lines between them, the actual geographic locations will form the outline of the seven-branch candlestick.

Throughout Revelation great emphasis is put upon the Son of Man figure and he is described by John in the opening monologue. "And from Jesus Christ, the faithful witness, first-born of the dead, and the ruler of kings on earth" (1:5a). John goes on to depict the Son of Man, Jesus Christ, as one "who loves us and has freed us from our sins by his blood and made us a kingdom, priests to his God and Father" (1:5-6). The choir then interjects the music, "Behold, he is coming with the clouds and every eye will see him, every one who pierced him; and all tribes of the earth will wail on account of him. Even so, Amen. 'I am the Alpha and the Omega,' says the Lord God, who is, who was, and the one who is to come, the Almighty" (1:7-8).

We are now ready for the first Act of our drama to begin. The Chorus is in place on the orchestra level. John stands on the ledge in front of the seven windows of the stage building. The dramatic scenes of the seven acts will be seen in these seven windows. As we begin Act I of the drama, be sure to keep the three codes of Revelation in mind and watch how John weaves these throughout the drama. John has just delivered the prologue (1:1-6) and the choir has responded (1:7-8). The stage is now prepared for Act I, The Seven Golden Lampstands.

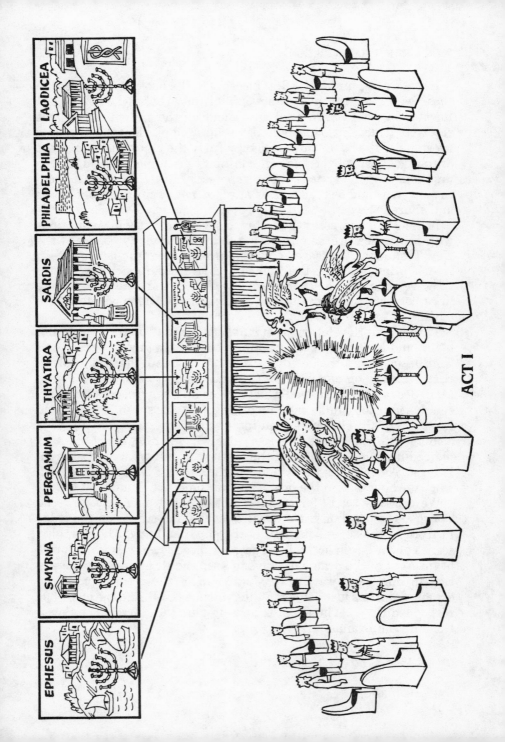

LAODICEA PHILADELPHIA SARDIS THYATIRA PERGAMUM SMYRNA EPHESUS

ACT I

Act I
The Seven Golden Lampstands

Revelation 1:9 to 3:22

Stage Setting

The action takes place on the ledge (*proskene*) before the seven great windows (*thuromata*) of the Ephesian stage. Seven golden lampstands stand on the stage, one in front of each of the seven windows. Each of these lampstands has seven branches (menorah). The Son of Man figure stands at the center of the stage and prepares to speak a message to each of the seven churches. These churches are symbolized by the lampstands. As each lamp is lighted, a painting of the city in which the church is located appears in the window behind the lampstand. The Son of Man speaks a message to each church as the lamp is lighted.

The Son of Man is dressed in the garments of a priest prepared to enter the Temple. The color code is very helpful in understanding this figure. His garments are white, a color which represents purity or conquering. Around his chest is a gold band or girdle; gold stands for worth or value. His feet are like brass, signifying strength or power. His hair is white, indicating, again, purity or conquering. His eyes are flaming fire, symbolizing his holiness. From his mouth comes a two-edged sword, representing the piercing nature of his words. Thus, John has preached a sermon entirely in colors. When decoded by Christians who were being persecuted, it had great meaning. The figure used here is also found in Daniel 7:13, where he is a divine man, coming on the clouds of heaven. The early Christians saw this figure as fulfilled in Christ. John combined the description of the Ancient of Days figure with that of the Son of Man, both in Daniel, and fashioned his high-priestly figure in Revelation. The result is a commanding divine figure who speaks a message to each of the churches receiving the Book of Revelation. Although one could not speak openly about Christ because of persecution, John's coded portrayal of him allowed the Christians to grasp something of his power and glory.

The Jewish Temple

Each of the stage settings in Revelation has some theme from the Jewish Temple in Jerusalem. In Act I the spotlight falls on the seven-branched lampstand of gold which stood inside the Holy Place of the Temple (Ex. 25:31-36). Other furnishings included an altar of incense and a table for the shewbread. In addition, the Son of Man is clothed as a priest ready to enter the Holy Place.

The Letters to the Seven Churches

The message in each of the seven letters to the churches in the Book of Revelation has seven major points.

1. **Words of greeting:**   Directed to the messenger or pastor of the church.
2. **Words from the Son of Man:**   Shows some reflection on the Son of Man figure from Revelation 1. This reflection is related to the history and background of the city receiving the letter.
3. **Words of praise:**   Shows some word of commendation for the people of that local church. John was a very wise man in expressing appreciation before turning to weaknesses.
4. **Words of weakness:**   All but two of the churches have very glaring weaknesses which are pointed out by John.
5. **Words of warning:**   A special warning is given to each church.
6. **Words of reward:**   A reward is granted to each church.
7. **Words of music:**   A hymn is sung by the choir at the orchestra level, "He who has an ear."

Sometimes points 6 and 7 are reversed in the letters. One lamp in the lampstand is lighted as each of the seven points is read aloud.

Scene 1
The First Golden Lampstand—Ephesus (2:1-7)

Stage Setting: The Son of Man lights the first lampstand. In the window behind the lampstand, a painting of the city of Ephesus appears. The Son of Man speaks a message to the church at Ephesus.

In each individual scene John repeats something about the Son of Man described in the stage setting of Act I and relates it in some way to the history of the city in question.

History: Jason, the first-century mayor of Ephesus, has consented to tell us of its history and give us a personal tour. (The names of the mayors in the seven cities are fictitious.)

JASON: Welcome to Ephesus, the great seaport of Asia Minor. Let me begin with a bit of our history. Legend has it that a group of Greek colonists went to the Delphi oracle to seek her wisdom in the founding of a new city. She related her assurances to the colonists that a fish and a wild boar would be their signs as they sought to locate the new settlement. They set sail on the Aegean Sea, looking for a suitable location. One evening they anchored their ship off the coast of Asia Minor and went ashore to cook their supper on the beach. As they were cooking the fish over the fire, one of the fish jumped out and landed in the bush; this, in turn, scared a wild boar that was hiding there and it ran away. The colonists remembered the words of the Delphi oracle. They proceeded to found the colony of Ephesus on that location. Whether that story has any validity, we do not know. However, these first Greek colonists came to the area around the eleventh century BC. They expelled the local inhabitants who had worshiped Cybele there for many centuries and built the city between the mountains of Koressos and Pion, some distance southeast of the Hellenic Ephesus. The Greek colonists over the next four centuries gradually changed from the worship of Athena to the veneration of Artemis, the goddess of the local Anatolian population. Their greatest accomplishment was the building of a huge temple to Artemis at the beginning of the sixth century BC. It was built on marshy ground to avoid damage from earthquakes. Historians in your day count this temple as one of the seven wonders of the ancient world.

In 560 BC Croesus, king of Lydia, conquered Ephesus and brought it under the control of Anatolian power. He added to the temple to Artemis by extending the sanctuary and introducing golden calves for its beautification. The population moved from the hillsides down to the temple area and constructed homes there. In 546 BC Ephesus came under control of Persia and was deemed a part of the satrapy of Ionia. During political upheaval and feuding in the area in 450 BC, the temple of Artemis was badly damaged. About a hundred years later, in 356 BC, it was burned to the ground by Herostratus, a madman looking for some way to write his name in history. Legend says that it was burned on the very night that Alexander the Great was born.

In 334 BC Alexander the Great conquered Persia at the Granicus River and Ephesus came under Macedonian power. The temple of Artemis was rebuilt to become again a very imposing structure. Let us stop and visit this temple. It is 425 feet long and 225 feet wide. There are 127 columns, sixty feet high, each constructed on its own pedestal. As you can see, thirty-six of these columns contain elaborate reliefs. A horseshoe-shaped altar, trimmed with marble, occupies the center of the temple. Over 1,000 sacred women serve in this temple.

Upon the death of Alexander the Great, Lysimachus became the ruler of Asia Minor and the city of Ephesus. He is often considered the founder of the modern city. A story is told that he built a wall around the present city. During his rule it was necessary to relocate the city, so a fourth Ephesus was built. The area of the third city was constantly being inundated by the river, with the whole area swampy and disease-ridden. After the new city was constructed, Lysimachus found that the people were reluctant to move into it, so he stopped up the storm sewers, flooded the old city, and the inhabitants were forced to take up residence in the new city. Lysimachus was defeated and slain by Seleucus I in 281 BC.

Seleucus I gave the kingdom to his son, Antiochus I, who then ruled over Ephesus. In 190 BC Seleucid king Antiochus III (the Great), was defeated by the Romans and the cities of Asia Minor fell under the dominion of Rome.

During the New Testament period which you are now visiting, the city has reached its golden age and become the leading city of Asia Minor. Ephesus is the main entry point to the Roman provinces and is a great seaport town of about 500,000 people. When Roman rulers visit in Asia Minor, the first port of call is always the city of Ephesus. The city is built on the Cayster River which provides many benefits and also some serious problems. During the rainy season of the springtime, the river floods and silts up the very narrow harbor leading into Ephesus from the Aegean Sea. Ephesus is a powerful, wealthy city with many beautiful buildings; however, our greatest attraction is the temple to Artemis. Another site of considerable note is the grand theater which we have already visited.

Thank you, Mayor Jason, for this tour.

Several hundred years after the New Testament period, the city lost its fight with the river, the harbor was permanently silted up, and now a grain field stands in its place. The ruins of Ephesus today are 4 to 5 miles from the Aegean Sea. From Ephesus, John, as the leader of the seven churches, could very easily visit the other cities in the province. It had become one of the first cities to practice Caesar worship with the largest statue of Caesar Domitian erected in its city square, a statue some 16 feet tall. In this cosmopolitan setting John directed his letter to the church at Ephesus.

The Message to Ephesus

Words of greeting.—A message is sent to the pastoral leader of Ephesus (2:1a).

Words from the Son of Man.—"The words of him who holds the seven stars in his right hand, who walks among the seven golden lampstands" (2:1b). John repeats what he has said about the Son of Man in 1:13,16. Ephesus was considered the central city of Asia Minor, with many Roman documents pointing to the fact that to say Ephesus was to say Asia Minor. As a major seaport area, all commerce coming into Asia Minor flowed through the port of Ephesus; so it is very fitting that John would again describe the Son of Man as standing in the midst of the lampstands just as Ephesus stood at the center of attention for the surrounding cities.

Words of praise.—"I know your works, your toil and your patient endurance, and how you cannot bear evil men but have tested those who call themselves apostles but are not and found them to be false; I know you are enduring patiently and bearing up for my name's sake, and you have not grown weary" (2:2-3). The emphasis is upon work and endurance. John is very happy to give the report that the church is an active one and is carrying out the work of Jesus Christ, not just a church filled with talk, but with action accompanying the witness. Over and over in verses 2 and 3 he emphasizes work, labor, endurance, bearing up and not fainting, all active words.

Words of weakness.—The basic criticism is that they have departed from their first love (2:4). This statement in verse 4 is directly related to the false teachers mentioned in verse 6. These false teachers are called Nicolaitans. In rooting out false teachers, the church had suffered in brotherly love. John, elsewhere in his letters, relates the fact that love of God and brotherly love are in close alignment one with another. One cannot say that he loves his brother and hate his fellowman. Thus, when brotherly love is affected in the church, one's love for God also suffers. False teachers had to be rooted out, but in the process damage had been done in the fellowship. The Spirit speaks through John in calling the people back to the high standards of love for one another and for God.

The Nicolaitans traced their history back to a man by the name of Nicholas who taught that the body and soul were distinct entities. Body or flesh was evil, and the soul was good. In this gnostic view no matter what one did in his body, it did not affect his soul. Many of these who had come into the church at Ephesus were teaching that it was fine to bow down to a statue of Caesar so that one could buy food for the family and, all the while, one could worship Christ. This was a very dangerous philosophy and also very attractive. One could worship Caesar and Christ. This group took the view that Christ was only an angel or messenger, bringing a password to earth. Once the password was discovered, one could escape the human body and be free to unite with God. John, then, was not upholding the false teachers, but he was pointing out the weakness of a broken fellowship which had resulted from rooting out the false teachers.

Words of warning.—"Remember then from what you have fallen, repent and do the work you did at first. If not, I will come upon you and remove your lampstand from its place, unless you repent" (2:5). The call is to do a complete about-face, repent. The warning emphasizes that the lampstand, which symbolizes the church, might be taken from its place, a very serious warning.

Words of music.—The choir: "He who has an ear, let him hear what the Spirit says to the churches" (2:7*a*). The choir on the orchestra level repeats this hymn after each letter is read aloud.

Words of reward.—"To him who conquers I will grant to eat of the tree of life, which is in the paradise of God" (2:7 *b*). A strong emphasis is placed upon the verb to conquer; Christians were expected to resist Caesar worship and press on, never giving up or surrendering. Those who achieved victory would be given the reward of eating from the tree of life in the paradise of God. The Bible begins with paradise and the tree of life and it ends in Revelation with paradise and tree of life. However, in Revelation the tree is open and available to all who have persevered.

Scene 2
The Second Golden Lampstand—Smyrna (2:8-11)

Stage Setting. The Son of Man lights the second lampstand. In the window behind the lampstand, a painting of the city of Smyrna is seen. The Son of Man speaks a message to the church.

History. Let us meet Alexander, first-century mayor of Smyrna who will tell us of its history and give us a tour.

ALEXANDER: Welcome to Smyrna, one of the most beautiful cities in the world. As you see, its majestic mountaintop setting provides a striking scene to those sailing into its fine harbor. Smyrna is over 1,000 years old. It began its history as an Ionian colony. About 600 BC the Greeks captured the city and destroyed it. In one sense Smyrna was dead. It would not come alive again until the third century BC. Under Alexander the Great, Smyrna was refounded as a city and became a striking example of the best of Hellenism. Alexander's successor, Lysimachus, continued to beautify Smyrna and make it into one of the jewels of Asia Minor. After the restoration of the city in 290 BC, Smyrna continued to flourish and become more important in the Roman period. From earliest times Smyrna counted itself an ally of Rome. It instituted the worship of Rome as early as 195 BC, when Syria was still a power to be considered. Cicero once said, "Smyrna is a city of our most faithful and most ancient allies."

Here in Smyrna we boast of being first of Asia in beauty and size. Much of the beauty is due to our city's orderly arrangement. You can see the streets (praised for the excellence of their paving) laid out in rectangular blocks. The crown of Smyrna is a well-known phrase in our world. This is a reference to the public buildings on top of Mount Pagos, our city's acropolis. The ancient writers speak of the great beauty of Smyrna. Aristides once described our city, "A statue, sitting with her feet on the sea, and her head rising to heaven, crowned with a circlet of beautiful buildings." He also mentioned our famous street of gold which runs through the temple of Zeus to the temple of Cybele, the mother goddess and patron of Smyrna. Sailing into the harbor of Smyrna, I hope you observed that the city walls atop Mount Pagos, along with the golden street linking the temples, gives the impression of a beautiful golden crown.

Our city is blessed with a wonderful climate and location. Western winds and its hilly location 2,500 feet above sea level keep the city cool in the summer. We also claim Smyrna as the birthplace of Homer, honoring him by placing his image on our coins and erecting a theater in his honor, The Homerion.

Thank you, Mayor Alexander, for the tour. Smyrna was the last of the seven cities to fall to the Eastern barbarians. It had the unique ability to pick itself up and rebuild. Even today there is a thriving, modern seaport still there, the city of Izmir.

The Message to Smyrna

Words of greeting.—A message is sent to the pastoral leader of the church at Smyrna (2:8a).

Words from the Son of Man.—"The words of the first and last, who died and came to life" (2:8b). As we have seen, the city of Smyrna was dead (from 600 to 290 BC), but was miraculously restored by King Lysimachus in 290 BC. The words about the Son of Man figure highlight this fact in the city's past: ". . . who died and came to life."

Words of praise.—"I know your tribulation and your poverty (but you are rich) and the slander of those who say they are Jews and are not, but are a synagogue of Satan" (2:9). The church of Smyrna was undergoing great persecution. It was the first of the cities in Asia Minor to practice the worship of Rome, and was proud of its Roman background. There is some evidence that the Jews in Smyrna participated with the Romans in beautifying the city and were proud of their special position with Rome. The Jewish community was very reluctant to have any identification with Christians. Many of the Christians in Smyrna were slaves, poor people, who did not have a very bright future in terms of their place in the city of Smyrna. John emphasizes the fact that Christians are the true people of God, the true Jews. He uses very strong language in calling the Jews of the city the synagogue of Satan.

Words of weakness.—There are no exact words of weakness for the church. It would seem that persecution brings out the best in people and in churches. Thus, there are no direct weaknesses apparent in the community of believers in Smyrna.

Words of warning.—John points out: "Behold, the devil is about to throw some of you into prison, that you may be tested, and for ten days you will have tribulation" (2:10). The tribulation will last ten days; ten in the number code means a complete period of time. One should not think of a literal ten days of tribulation, but rather a complete period of persecution, tribulation, and suffering would be confronted by the church.

Words of reward.—Just as a crown of beautiful buildings and a golden street bedecked the hill of Smyrna, so also the Christians will receive the crown of life. John alludes to the city's most famous aspect, the great crown that one could see sailing into the harbor. But an even greater spiritual crown will be attained by the Christians who persevere. They will also not be harmed by the second death. In Revelation the second death is the lake of fire into which Satan and his helpers and unbelievers are cast at the end of the age. The members of the church receive the great promise that they will be secure in the hands of God.

Words of music.—The choir on the orchestra level sings the hymn once again, "He who has an ear, let him hear what the Spirit says to the churches" (2:11).

Scene 3
The Third Golden Lampstand—Pergamum (2:12-17)

Stage Setting: The Son of Man lights the third lampstand and in the panel behind the lampstand a painting of the city of Pergamum appears. The Son of Man speaks a message to the church at Per-

gamum. This city, the capital city of Asia Minor, was called the city
of the sword.

History: Let us meet Mayor Pliny, the first-century mayor of
Pergamum, who will tell us of the history of this area and give us
a guided tour.

PLINY: Welcome to Pergamum, a city built on a hill. Our hill dominates the plain of Caicus and our city's history goes back to the
fifth century BC. Pergamum, however, emerged as a major power
in 282 BC when Philetaerus revolted against Lysimachus and
founded the kingdom of Pergamum. Our city fell under Syrian
control in 222 BC, when Antiochus the Great conquered it. In 190
BC Pergamum came under control of the Romans and was made
the capital of the new province of Asia.

We are proud to say that the first temple of the imperial cult
involving the worship of Rome in Asia was built in Pergamum in
29 BC. This temple appears on almost all the coins of the city. Our
city has four favorite deities: Zeus, Athena, Dionysus, and Asklepios. The first two represent the Greek influence; the last two
show the Anatolian influence.

Pergamum is situated about fifteen miles inland from the
Aegean Sea on the Caicus River. Most of the city is built on a hill
1,000 feet high. On this hill is located the famous library of Pergamum, second only to Alexandria. Your English word *parchment*
comes from the word *Pergamum.* Ours is one of the first cities to
use city planning. Public buildings are at the top of the hill; the
residential area for the rich is just below the public buildings; the
marketplace then separates the rich from the poor residents at the
foot of the hill. On the top of the hill stands the library, the famous
altar to Zeus, many public temples, and a beautiful amphitheater
that goes down the side of the hill. At the foot of the mountain is
the famous medical school, named in honor of the god Asklepios.
People from all over Asia Minor come here to seek healing. The
mile-long entranceway leads to the medical school and is lined
with statues of parts of human bodies that have been healed at the
school, with an eye, a nose, a big foot, an ear punctuating the
entranceway. Patients enter the school, are quizzed about their
ailments, and then are led down a dark hallway to a sleeping room
where they are given a strong wine to drink. We believe that

during the night the god Asklepios reveals to them the nature of their ailments and the cures.

The medical school covers several acres, including an amphitheater, athletic field, and other places of entertainment for the patients. Several other temples are also included in the medical school complex. The symbol for the school is the intertwining snakes. This goes back to a legend about a man who had come to be healed at the medical school, had not been made well, and on his way out found two snakes fighting over a bowl of milk. He thought that he was doomed to death anyway, so he picked up the poisoned milk and drank it, and immediately he became well.

Pergamum is the capital city of Asia Minor, with the power to have its own local assembly and even to pass the death penalty. We are directly under the control of the Roman senate and, as such, have the power of the sword. Our location on the mountaintop makes us a strong city and we have resisted many enemy attacks successfully.

Thank you, Mayor Pliny, for those words.

The Message to Pergamum

Words of greeting.—A message is given to the pastoral leader of the church in Pergamum (2:12*a*).

Words from the Son of Man.—"The words of him who has the sharp two-edged sword" (2:12*b*). The theme from the Son of Man reemphasizes the sharp two-edged sword in the mouth of the Son of Man figure mentioned previously in 1:16. It seemed that Pergamum was called the city of the sword because the local senate had the power to pass the death penalty. The spotlight falls on the sword in the mouth of the Son of Man. The message is that the sword of the Son of Man is far superior to that of the famous sword in Pergamum.

Words of praise.—John again emphasizes work and labor. "I know where you dwell, where Satan's throne is; you hold fast my name and you did not deny my faith even in the days of Antipas, my witness" (2:13). Stress is placed here upon the famous altar of Zeus that was on top of the mountain in Pergamum. The church had persevered, even in the face of persecution. According to church tradition, a young teenager, Antipas, had been put to death by being boiled alive in hot oil in the city square in Pergamum. It would have been very difficult for the church to persevere in face of this great persecution. Antipas is called my faithful witness; the word *martus* is used here, from which we get our word *martyr*.

Words of weakness.—"But I have a few things against you: you have some there who hold the teaching of Balaam, who taught Balak to put a stumbling block before the sons of Israel, that they might eat food sacrificed to idols and practice immorality" (2:14). The weakness in the church had to do with the false teachers who had appeared in Pergamum and joined the church. John went back to the Old Testament Book of Numbers to point out a weakness now present in the church at Pergamum. In Numbers 31:16 and 25:1-2, we read the story of Balaam and Balak. The Jewish people were encamped on the east side of the Jordan River before moving into the Promised Land. There the Israelites were tempted to participate in fertility cults of the Canaanites. The emphasis in the story is placed upon giving in to idols and the worship of idols. The Nicolaitans are mentioned again in 2:15 and we would suppose then that they are directly related to the problem mentioned in 2:14. As we encountered them in Ephesus, we found them teaching that what one did in the body did not affect the soul. It was permissible to eat food that had been offered to idols, to participate in the fertility cults of Artemis, and to bow down to Caesar's statue. It was very fitting, then, to compare this to the Balaam and Balak situation in the Old Testament.

Words of warning.—"Repent then. If not, I will come to *you* soon and war against *them* with the sword of my mouth" (2:16). The theme returns to the sword which is symbolic of the city of Pergamum and also the strength and power of the Son of Man. The call is for repentance. The church should leave the teachings of the false disciples and return again to the example of young men such as Antipas who gave up his life rather than participate in Caesar worship.

Words of music.—"He who has an ear, let him hear what the Spirit says to the churches" (2:17a).

Words of reward.—"To him who conquers I will give some of the hidden manna, and I will give him a white stone, with a new name written on the stone which no one knows except him who receives it" (2:17 b). In Pergamum the people were proud of their free election of the local senate, voting for a candidate by casting in a white stone, voting against a candidate by casting a black stone. The athletic games often used the white stone as the price of admission. To receive a white stone with one's name written upon it would emphasize and symbolize acceptance by God. In the ancient Christian church when one became a Christian, often his name would be changed and he would receive a new Christian name. The Jewish people expected that the hidden manna would be revealed in the day of the Messiah. The manna which Moses had saved from the desert sojourn had been hidden away for the day the Messiah would return. The emphasis is upon the Christian people being the inheritors of that promise, receiving the manna or the Word of God.

Scene 4
The Fourth Golden Lampstand—Thyatira (2:18-29)

Stage Setting: The Son of Man lights the fourth lampstand. Behind the lampstand a painting of the city of Thyatira appears. The Son of Man speaks a message to the church at Thyatira.

History: Let us meet Lactanius, first-century mayor of Thyatira.

LACTANIUS: Welcome to our city. Thyatira is thought by some to be the least important of the seven cities, because it is a working-man's town. We feel it is quite important. It lies on the road between Pergamum and Sardis to the south on the banks of the Lycus River. This route is the most important road in the whole country, the one great way from Pergamum to the east. Thyatira has no natural protection; however, we guard the main road leading to the capital city of Pergamum.

Our city was founded by Seleucus I in 282 BC. Our residents worship the god Tyrimos, similar to the great god Apollo. He appears on our coins as a figure on horseback, armed with a battle-ax and fob. Thyatira is a great commercial center with more trade guilds located here than in any other Asian city. We have many kinds of workers, tanners, potters, bakers, slave dealers, bronze smiths. Lydia, mentioned in your Book of Acts (16:14), is from this city and is involved in selling purple cloth. As you walk through the city of Thyatira, you can see blazing ovens for making bronze and brass objects. We are the Pittsburgh of Asia Minor.

Thank you, Mayor Lactanius.

Thyatira experienced a history of constant destruction and rebuilding. Its unique position as a guardian city for the capital ensured its life. Even the conqueror felt constrained to rebuild in order to protect the newly acquired capital of Pergamum.

The Message to Thyatira

Words of greeting.—A message is given to the pastoral leader of the church at Thyatira (2:18a).

Words from the Son of Man.—"The words of the Son of God, who has eyes like a flame of fire, and whose feet are like burnished bronze" (2:18b). John repeats the stage theme from 1:14-15 concerning the Son of Man figure. His blazing eyes would remind the local inhabitants of the blazing furnaces of Thyatira. His bronze feet would suggest one of the primary products for which the city was known.

Words of praise.—"I know your works, your love and faith and service and patient endurance, and that your latter works exceed the first" (2:19). The church at Thyatira was a hardworking church and reflected the hard manual work for which the city was known. In contrast to the Ephesian church, their last works were even more significant than the first works. The church was a growing church, reaching out and expanding.

Words of weakness.—"But I have this against you, that you tolerate the woman Jezebel, who calls herself a prophetess and is teaching and beguiling my servants to practice immorality and to eat food sacrificed to idols. I gave her time to repent, but she refuses to repent of her immorality" (2:20-21). In Thyatira a false teacher had appeared in the form of a prophetess. We do not know who this Jezebel might have been. In fact, it is probably a symbolic name. Jezebel was one of the most wicked characters in the Old Testament. Ahab of the Northern Kingdom of Israel had married a Phoenician wife named Jezebel. She brought with her into the Northern Kingdom the worship of Baal from the land of Phoenicia. This worship involved sexual rites centering in a fertility cult. Many of the Israelites deserted the worship of Jahweh to adopt the fertility rites centered in the high places in the countryside. The prophet Elijah fought against Baal worship. In the famous encounter on Mount Carmel, he defeated hundreds of the prophets and Baal worship suffered as a result. This woman leader in the church was perhaps a member of the Nicolaitan party, encouraging the people to participate in sexual rites in the local worship centers, eat meat offered to idols, even to worship at the statue of Caesar Domitian.

Words of warning.—"Behold I will throw her on a sickbed, and those who commit adultery with her I will throw into great tribulation, unless they repent of her doings; and I will strike her children dead. And all the churches will know that I am he who searches mind and heart" (2:22-23). Her children (2:23) would be her followers. There is a strong warning that this false teaching must be blotted out of the church. As a result of God's judgment, all the churches will know that he is the one who searches out the innermost feelings of the individual. Kidneys and heart are the actual words in verse 23, going back to the Jewish practice of assigning special feelings to different organs of the body. In our American culture we put great emphasis upon the heart as the center of emotion, especially the emotion of love. In the ancient world the thought process or center of logic was in the heart, a man thought in his heart. The kidneys, as well as the gallbladder, were thought to be the place of evil feelings. The source of emotion, especially love, was considered to be the intestines. Thus, the emphasis here is searching out the innermost parts of one's life. Again, importance is placed on works.

Words of reward.—"I will give him power over the nations, . . . and I will give him the morning star" (2:26,28). In verses 24-28 John gives us a rather extensive reward for the church. Those who have not participated in these beliefs of the false teachers, who have not shared in the deep secrets of Satan, will not have any other burden placed upon them. The deep secrets of Satan mentioned in 2:34 would be a reference to some of the mystery cults and fertility rites which were very prominent in the city of Pergamum. They also were given authority over the nations to rule them with an iron rod. This promise originally had been given to the Jews in the Old Testament (see Ps. 2:8-9) that they would rule over the Gentiles. Now the promise is reversed and the Gentile Christians will rule over the world. In verse 28 a morning star symbolizes the Messiah. The great reward and ultimate gift for this working church was the Messiah himself.

Words of music.—"He who has an ear, let him hear what the Spirit says to the church" (2:29).

Scene 5
The Fifth Golden Lampstand—Sardis (3:1-6)

Stage Setting: The Son of Man lights the fifth lampstand; in the window behind the lampstand a painting of the city of Sardis appears. The Son of Man speaks a message to the church at Sardis.

History: Let us meet Mayor Celsius of Sardis who will tell us of their history and guide us through the city.

CELSIUS: Welcome to Sardis known for its mountaintop location and its failure to be on guard throughout its history. Sardis has suffered several military defeats by sneak attack. It is one of the outstanding cities of ancient history; located on a plateau 1,500 feet above sea level, it was an ideal situation to defend. The word *Sardis* is a plural word in Greek, indicating two cities, a lower city and an upper city. The upper city is built on Mount Tmolus. In time of warfare and seige the whole population retreats to the mountaintop. Mount Tmolus is like a watchtower, overlooking the Hermus plain. The history of Sardis goes back to about 1200 BC at the beginning of the Lydian kingdom. The city quickly outgrew its mountaintop location and a lower city was built at the foot of the mountain. The old city then served as a fortress. As capital of ancient Lydia, Sardis is a very wealthy city; perhaps because of this it had to fight frequent battles. The Greek cities along the coast have always viewed Sardis as the enemy. Its very name stands for power, wealth, and great force.

Back in 546 BC the fall of Sardis was earthshaking news in the world. Croesus, King of Sardis, had consulted all the Greek gods and the Delphi oracle before he went to war with Cyrus of Persia. He crossed the Halys into Persia and was crushed by Cyrus. He retreated back to Sardis to build up an army for the next year. Cyrus surprised everyone by following the Lydians to Sardis and laying seige to the city. King Croesus thought that he now had Cyrus where he wanted him. He retired one night, thinking all was well, and awakened the next morning to find Cyrus in control of the acropolis. The rock which underlaid the city was limestone and very porous, a type of material which cracks and erodes easily. Cyrus found such a spot and led his soldiers under the city wall into the heart of the city. For lack of proper care, this weakness had gone unnoticed by the officials of Sardis; however, the wise Persians were looking for such a flaw. The people of Sardis were so confident of the impossibility of attack from the steep mountain side of the city that they did not even post a guard there.

History was repeated and the same thing happened again in 230 BC when Antiochus the Great of Persia captured Sardis by coming up the unguarded mountainside of the city. As before, all the soldiers were stationed on the southern wall of the city, the easiest approach to Sardis.

The patron goddess of our city is Cybele, whose fertility cult involves the worship of nature. Cybele is thought to have the power of restoring life to the dead. We experienced a harsh earthquake in AD 17, but recovered with generous help from the Roman emperor, Tiberius. During the Roman period the upper city gradually ceased to be part of the true city since it was too inconvenient.

Thank you, Mayor Celsius, for the tour.

The Message to Sardis

Words of greeting.—A message is addressed to the pastoral leader of the church at Sardis (3:1a).

Words from the Son of Man.—"The words of him who has the seven spirits of God and the seven stars" (3:1a). John calls us back to the description of the Son of Man given in 1:16 as the one who has the seven stars in his right hand. In its mountaintop location the lights of Sardis could be seen across the whole plain; correlating with the stars in the hands of the Son of Man.

Words of praise.—"Yet you have still a few names in Sardis, people who have not soiled their garments" (3:4). John indicates that there were a few in the city who had not soiled their garments by participating in idol worship. There is very little to be found of praise in this letter. The church is obviously very weak and near the point of extinction.

Words of weakness.—This theme is much more extensive in the letter to the church at Sardis. "I know your works; you have the name of being alive, and you are dead" (3:1). Just like the city, the church could look back to former days when it had been stronger and given a better witness to the Lord. Now it had grown weak. The work of the church was not complete or fulfilled before God, as John points out in verse 2.

Words of warning.—"Awake" (2:2). Great emphasis is put upon the background of being watchful or awake because the city had been taken by stealth two times in its history. Cyrus the Great and Antiochus the Great had come into the city because of the failure to guard and watch. The church also must guard itself and become stronger or it too will pass away. Thus, in 3:3 John enjoins them to remember what they have received and heard. "If you will not awake, I will come like a thief [just like Cyrus the Great], and you will not know at what hour I will come upon you" (3:3).

Words of reward.—"He who conquers shall be clad thus in white garments, and I will not blot his name out of the book of life; I will confess his name before my father and before his angels" (3:5). White clothing was a sign of the immortal body which would be received at the last day. Jewish people had adopted the Book of Life from the Persians. In Persian cities one could find a list of all tax-paying citizens in a book called the book of the living. In the Jewish context the book contained a list of the kingdom of God. In Revelation there is such a book that is opened at the final judgment, containing the names of all true believers; those who persevered and conquered will not have their names removed from this book.

Words of music.—"He who has an ear, let him hear what the Spirit says to the churches" (3:6).

Scene 6
The Sixth Golden Lampstand—Philadelphia (3:7-13)

Stage Setting: The Son of Man lights the sixth lampstand; in the window behind the lampstand a painting of the city of Philadelphia appears. The Son of Man speaks a message to the church of Philadelphia.

History: Let us meet Gregory, first-century mayor of Philadelphia, who will guide us through his city.

GREGORY: Welcome to Philadelphia, best known as an open door for the entrance of Greek culture to the barbarian world. This city was named after Attalus II, 159-138 BC, and was called Philadelphus because of his love for his brother, Eumenes II. It was located in the valley of the Cogamus River, a tributary of the Hermus. Philadelphia was founded by one of the other seven cities, Pergamum. The leaders of that city wanted to found a community on the frontier of their kingdom to consolidate, regulate, and educate the barbarians. They particularly desired to import Greek culture. It was very successful. By AD 19 Greek was spoken in the area and the Lydian language was in disuse. The main road from Smyrna runs along the side of the Cogamus River, past Philadelphia, and on to the east. Our city is located on a broad hill running from the river up to Mount Tmolus. The city of Philadelphia was destroyed by a terrible earthquake in AD 17 and tremors continue in and around the city even to our time. You will notice that many of our citizens are living outside the city wall in tents and huts, refusing to reenter the city.

Thank you, Mayor Gregory, for the tour. In the fourteenth century Philadelphia stood alone as a Christian city against the Turkish power. Finally the Turks took the city in 1379 to 1390 and it became the Muslim town of Alasehir, meaning the reddish city.

The Message to Philadelphia

Words of greeting.—A message is addressed to the pastoral leader of the church at Philadelphia (3:7).

Words from the Son of Man.—"The words of the holy one, the true one, who has the key of David, who opens and no one shall shut, who shuts and no one opens" (3:7*b*). Those words had been used to describe the Son of Man in 1:4,18. Now they are applied to the church at Philadelphia. Throughout the letter John made great use of the symbol of the door. The city had been built there to be an open door to the barbarians, to teach them Greek culture. Now the church had an open door before it. It possessed the keys of David to open and to close.

Words of praise.—"I know your works. Behold I have set before you an open door, which no one is able to shut. I know that you have but little power and yet you have kept my word and have not denied my name" (3:8). Next to the church at Smyrna, Philadelphia was the strongest of the seven churches. Much emphasis is placed here upon works and keeping the word of God. Even though existing in a frontier city, the Christian church was able to proclaim the name of Jesus Christ to the barbarians.

Words of weakness.—There are no words of weakness as such to this church. The only possible reference to weakness would be the use of the adjective *little* in 3:8, "you have but little power." Perhaps there was some room for the church to expand and grow in terms of its spiritual might and power.

Words of warning.—"I am coming soon; hold fast what you have, so that no one may seize your crown" (3:11). There is no direct warning to the church at Philadelphia, yet there is an injunction to be loyal and true to the end. "Behold I will make those of the synagogue of Satan who say they are Jews and are not, but lie—behold I will make them come and bow down before your feet, and learn that I have loved you" (3:9). Even as in Smyrna, perhaps the Jews of Philadelphia had participated with the Romans in persecuting the Christians. Again, John has very strong words of warning for these people.

Words of reward.—"Because you have kept my word of patient endurance, I will keep you from the hour of trial which is coming upon the whole world to try those dwelling upon the earth" (3:10). This statement was a direct reference to the persecution of Caesar Domitian that was spreading across the countryside. An important and interesting reward is found in verse 12a, "I will make him a pillar in the temple of my god; never shall he go out of it." Church members who were living outside the city in tents or huts because of the earth tremors could envision no greater reward than to be a pillar in the Temple of God and never have to go outside the city again. Another aspect of the reward will be that "I will write on him the name of my God, the new Jerusalem which comes down from my God out of heaven, and my own new name" (3:12b). This is a clear assurance of God's concern and constant care for the church.

Words of music.—"He who has an ear, let him hear what the Spirit says to the churches" (3:13).

Scene 7
The Seventh Golden Lampstand—Laodicea (3:14-22)

Stage Setting: The Son of Man lights the seventh lampstand; in the window behind the lampstand is pictured the city of Laodicea. The Son of Man speaks a message to the church at Laodicea.

History: Let us meet Manean, first-century governor of Laodicea.

MANEAN: Welcome to our beautiful city on the Lycus River. Our city is the wealthiest of the seven and is well known for its banking industry, its manufacture of woolen cloth, and its medical school which produces eye salve. Laodicea was founded by Antiochus II in 261-246 BC. The great road to the east from Ephesus runs through the city. Antiochus named the city after his beloved wife, Laodice. It is located in the Lycus River Valley, directly across the river from Hierapolis and 12 miles downstream from another biblical city, Colossae. The city was built to guard the main road to the East; however, we have an inadequate supply of water in time of seige. We are best known in the Roman world for banking and manufacturing; the Lycus Valley is also famous for its sheep and their soft, glossy black wool, used in the manufacture of a popular line of clothing.

Laodicea has a famous temple to the Phrygian god, Men Karou. A well-known school of medicine is connected with this temple. These Laodicean physicians follow the teachings of Herophilus, 330-250 BC. An eye salve, known all over the Roman world, is produced at the school.

We have a large Jewish population, approximately 7,500. Our city has to struggle constantly to overcome its lack of water. In earlier times an aqueduct was built to bring water to the city from hot springs; these springs are about 95 degrees. By the time the water reaches us, it is only lukewarm. Unfortunately, because of this, our water is neither therapeutically hot nor refreshingly cold.

Thank you, Mayor Manean, for the tour.

The Message to Laodicea

Words of greeting.—A message is addressed to the pastoral leader of the church at Laodicea (3:14).

Words from the Son of Man.—"The words of the Amen, the faithful and true witness, the beginning of God's creation" (3:14*b*). John repeats what he has said about the Son of Man in 1:5. Laodicea was by far the most important and wealthiest of the seven cities and many of the inhabitants certainly would declare that it was the beginning of the creation. John wants to emphasize the Son of Man figure is far more important than anything that could be found in the city.

Words of praise.—There was little in this church to praise. Perhaps the wealth of the city had overwhelmed the members of the church.

Words of weakness.—The major weakness has to do with the lukewarm nature of the work of the church. "I know your works; you are neither cold nor hot" (3:15*a*). The church is just like the city's water supply! "Would that you were cold or hot! So, because you are lukewarm, neither cold nor hot, I will spew you out of my mouth" (3:15 *b*-16). One of the strongest words in Revelation is used here, *emesai,* meaning to vomit.

Words of warning.—The warning emphasizes the three reasons for Laodicea's fame: money, clothing, and medicine. Instead of real gold, one should seek spiritual treasures. Instead of the famous cloth of Laodicea, one should seek to put on spiritual clothing. Instead of the eye salve of the medical school, one should seek to put on spiritual medicine for the eyes.

Words of reward.—The greatest reward offered is to the weakest church. "He who conquers, I will grant him to sit with me on my throne" (3:21). A great reward is offered to the believers if they repent and share in the reign of Christ and the Father in the last day. The call is made at the end of the letter to behold Christ standing at the door and knocking. If anyone would open the door, he would come in and dine with the church.

Words of music.—"He who has an ear, let him hear what the Spirit says to the churches" (3:22).

Act I comes to an end with seven beautiful golden lampstands burning in the windows and seven impressive paintings of the cities behind them. We have heard and visualized a dramatic message in word and song from the Son of Man to the churches.

These messages to the seven churches are not just lessons in history. The church in every age has found comfort and help through these eternal messages. From Ephesus, we have heard the admonition to love God with the fullness of our being. The valiant witnesses of Smyrna have reminded us of the need to persevere and overcome. The Pergamum message has brought to mind the need to be aware of the dangers of false teachers. Thyatira has given us opportunity to think of our faith in reference to our life-style. The message to Sardis has caused us to understand the need to be watchful and carry forth good works for Christ. Philadelphia stands as a symbol of an open door of ministry available to the church in every age. Laodicea has set forth a picture of a contented, lukewarm church in the midst of wealth.

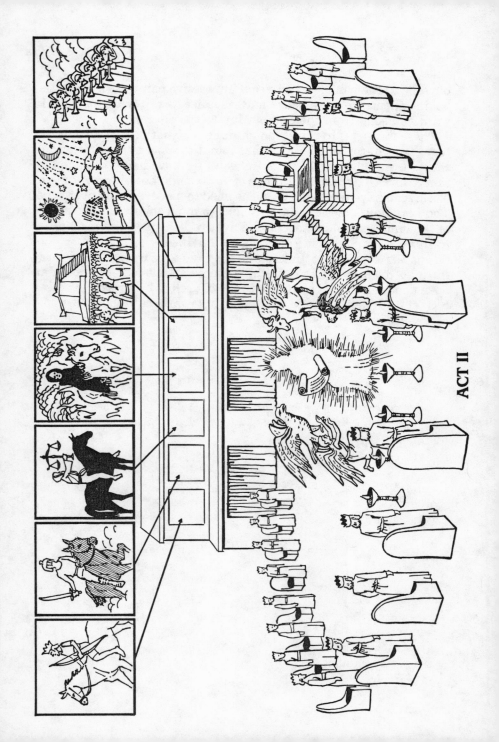

ACT II

Act II
The Seven Seals

Revelation 4:1 to 8:4

Stage Setting

In 4:1 John is caught up to heaven to behold the throne room of God. In this act a chorus of twenty-four elders will be featured. The stage setting is punctuated by five beautiful hymns, an act of worship and music. These hymns in Revelation have inspired great composers over the years. Two whole chapters, 4 and 5, are devoted to setting the stage for this great act. John declares in 4:1-2, "After this I looked, and lo, in heaven an open door! And the first voice, which I had heard speaking to me like a trumpet, said, 'Come up hither and I will show you what must take place after this.' At once I was in the Spirit, and lo, a throne stood in heaven." In the next two chapters John describes the stage setting. The spotlight is on the orchestra level of the stage of Ephesus.

The throne of God stands on the center of the stage. Around the throne of God are twenty-four small thrones. In verses 2-3 John describes the throne of God and the one seated upon it. Being a good Jew, John makes no attempt to describe the form of God, since Jews believe that God is a spirit. He describes the throne with lightning, bright lights, so as to blind human eyes; one cannot behold the form of God. The throne of God plays a significant role all the way through the Book of Revelation. It is mentioned in every chapter except 9 and 10. John uses such descriptive jewels as jasper, carnelian, and emerald. In the Old Testament these three precious stones represent the tribes of Reuben, Benjamin, and Judah. One cannot see the actual form on the throne; these sparkling jewels blind the viewers' eyes.

Around the throne is a dark green rainbow. In our color code dark green or emerald green represents eternal life. This whole stage setting in Revelation 4 and 5 becomes a living sermon, punctuated by color and music. John then describes in 4:4 and following the

49

twenty-four elders who are seated around the throne of God, dressed
in white clothing, with golden crowns upon their heads. Each elder
holds a harp. Just as in Greek tragic drama, the chorus of twenty-
four elders is very important for the rest of our drama. They sing and
interpret what is happening on the main stage. John's description
presents a majestic setting. Thunder and lightning and voices come
out of the throne. In front of the throne are seven burning torches.
John tells us these are the seven spirits of God. Throughout the
Bible, fire is a symbol for God's spirit. Moses beheld God in the
burning bush; a pillar of fire led the children of Israel out of Egypt.
In so many of the prophetic visions fire played a very significant role.
At Pentecost in Acts 2, tongues of fire were seen on the heads of the
disciples. The Holy Spirit came upon the group, thus the burning
torches represent the Holy Spirit. Seven in the number code represents divinity or holiness and fire symbolizes the Spirit of God.

Separating heaven from earth is the sea of glass. In the stage at
Ephesus there was a moat around the lower orchestra level that
could be flooded with water to present lakes, streams, or seas. In
actually dramatizing the book, the moat of water can be flooded to
represent the sea of glass. In the Book of Genesis, one reads that God
divided the earthly sea and the heavenly sea by a firmament.
Throughout Jewish literature there is mention of a heavenly sea.
John seems to have this in mind in the stage setting for Act II.

Around the throne of God and guarding the throne are four living
creatures. They are filled with eyes before and behind. The first
living creature is a lion; the second, an ox; the third, the face of a
man; the fourth, like a flying eagle. They each have six wings. These
four living creatures represent God's creation. The lion symbolizes
all the wild creatures, the ox all the domesticated creatures, the one
with the human face mankind, and the eagle all the flying creatures.
God is surrounded by his creation. That creation is imperfect so each
creature has six wings (six represents imperfection in the number
code). They do not cease giving praise to God both day and night. The
twenty-four elders, the choir, represent God's revelation of himself
to his creation, the Old Covenant and the New Covenant, the twelve
tribes of Israel, and the twelve disciples. Here we have a living
sermon, God surrounded by his creation and God's word to his creation. Later in the Book of Revelation when the new Jerusalem

comes down from heaven, the names of the twelve disciples are upon
the stones in the foundation of the city and the names of the twelve
tribes are upon the gates of the city. All in all, we behold a very
majestic scene.

At this point the first music begins in Act II. In our previous act
the choir had sung "He who has an ear, let him hear what the Spirit
says to the churches." In the beginning of Act II we have five musical
hymns. The hymns begin softly and gradually get louder until the
whole stage is shaking with the power of the music in the final fifth
hymn in chapter 5. The five hymns are: 4:8; 4:11; 5:9-10; 5:12; 5:13.

The first hymn begins in 4:8:

> Holy, holy, holy, is the Lord God Almighty,
> who was and is and is to come.

The four living creatures begin singing very softly around the throne
of God. This hymn proclaims the majesty of God. Then the twenty-
four elders fall on their faces before the throne of God, casting their
crowns before him, and begin the second hymn in 4:11.

> Worthy are thou our Lord and God,
> to receive glory and honor and power,
> for thou didst create all things
> and by thy will they existed and were created.

The second hymn is a hymn of praise to the Creator God.

At this point John notices a scroll in the hand of one who is seated
upon the throne. It is sealed in the front and on the back with seven
seals. The scroll gives its name to the whole act. As each of the seven
seals are broken, we will see action on the stage. An angel asks who
is worthy to open the scroll and loose its seals. No one could be found
in heaven or on earth or under the earth to open the scroll. John
begins to cry and an angel says, "Lo, the Lion of the tribe of Judah,
the Root of David, . . . can open the scroll" (5:5). Suddenly John
beholds a lamb standing on center stage. This is the first use of the
animal code. The lamb has seven horns representing divine power,
seven eyes, divine seeing. The lamb also had been slain which would
represent the crucified Christ to all Christians. An actor dressed in
black would carry a banner with the lamb emblazoned on it.

The twenty-four elders join the four living creatures and sing the
third hymn in 5:9. It is a hymn to the Lamb.

> Worthy are thou to take the scroll and to open its seals,
> for thou wast slain and by thy blood didst ransom men for God
> from every tribe and tongue and people and nation,
> and hast made them a kingdom and priests to our God
> and they shall reign on earth.

This is a hymn to the redemptive work of the Lamb. Thousands of angels come out from the side stage to join with the twenty-four elders and four living creatures in singing the fourth hymn in 5:12.

> Worthy is the Lamb who was slain, to receive power and wealth and wisdom and might and honor and glory and blessing!

Notice that in this hymn John makes use of a sevenfold pattern of music, his favorite all the way through the book. In the final hymn the chorus is swelled as millions of people in earth, under the earth, and in heaven join in the final musical selection, a song of praise to God and the Lamb, 5:13.

> To him who sits upon the throne and to the Lamb be blessing and honor and glory and might forever and ever!

The four living creatures declare Amen, let it be so. The elders fall upon their faces again and worship.

The stage setting in chapters 4 and 5 is very powerful, filled with the sheer beauty of music and poetry and worship. As the music swells, shaking the stage, the lamb walks out, takes the scroll, and breaks open the first of the seven seals. The seal visions appear in the seven windows on the stage at Ephesus.

The Jewish Temple

Each of the seven acts of Revelation stresses some theme from the Jewish Temple. In Act I, it was the menorah or seven-branch lampstand which stood in the Holy Place of the Temple. In Act II the spotlight will be on the Altar of Sacrifice which stood directly in front of the main Temple building.

Scene 1
The First Seal Vision—The White Horse (6:1-2)

Now I saw when the lamb opened one of the seven seals, and I heard one of the four living creatures say, as with a voice of thunder, "Come!" And I saw, and behold, a white horse and, its rider had a bow; and a crown was given to him, and he went out conquering and to conquer.

The white horse symbolizes conquering. In the color code white is the color for conquering. John wants to show us the course of human history. In every age people will set out to conquer the world; this whole act is cyclical in nature. The Greeks viewed history as a cycle, turning around and around, bringing the same events over and over again. Yet in Revelation, even as the cycles turn, we are moving forward toward a goal in history. In every age there will be world conquerors. The white horse appears on the human stage over and over again. In the ancient world there was Caesar Domitian, then Napoleon, Hitler, Stalin, and so it will go until the end of history. Symbolic of conquering is the crown which is given to the rider of the white horse. Also the bow in his hands stands for the power of armies sweeping across the face of the earth.

Christians reading Revelation in the first century surely would have visualized the nation of Parthia. These people were the ancient enemies of the Romans. In fact, Rome was never able to conquer Parthia whose soldiers were very adept at using the bow and arrow and not only could fire forward but also could turn while riding their horses and fire over their shoulders. This made them a very dangerous foe. From John, the Parthian hordes symbolized the conquerors down through world history, right across the pages of time.

Scene 2
The Second Seal Vision—The Red Horse (6:3-4)

When he opened the second seal, I heard the second living creature say, "Come!" And out came another horse, bright red; its rider was permitted to take peace from the earth, so that men should slay one another; and he was given a great sword.

Following the horse of conquering, one might well expect the red horse of warfare. Jesus himself spoke of "wars and rumors of wars" (Mark 13:7). Wars have punctuated the history of mankind on the face of the earth and will continue to do so until the end of the age. In the color code red symbolizes warfare. The rider is given a sword.

The Greek word for *sword* indicates the short Roman sword invented by the Roman army for hand-to-hand combat. First-century Christians would have viewed this in terms of the mighty Roman army which had marched across the Mediterranean world, slaying with the sword, putting people into subjection, and now conquering the Christians. They held Asia Minor in a firm grasp. Every age has experienced the peril of war, the modern age perhaps more than any other age.

Scene 3
The Third Seal Vision—The Black Horse (6:5-6)

When he opened the third seal, I heard the third living creature say "Come!" And I saw, and behold, a black horse, and its rider had a balance in his hand; and I heard what seemed to be a voice in the midst of the four living creatures saying, "A quart of wheat for a denarius and three quarts of barley for a denarius; but do not harm oil and wine."

Following conquering and warfare, one might expect the third horse to be the black horse of famine. Black in the color code symbolizes famine. The scourge of every major war is the blight of hunger and famine which spreads across the face of the land. The first-century people were well aware of the horrible periods of famine in many parts of their world. The voice proclaims the extent of the famine. One quart of wheat costs a denarius or twenty cents. In the first century workers were hired at sunup in the marketplace, worked twelve hours until sundown, for the working man's wage of twenty cents. Sometimes the laborers stood in the marketplace and were not hired, that night families would not eat. Life was a day-by-day experience. At the end of the day the landowner did not even have to pay the worker his wage. There were no courts to which the laborers might take the landowner. The ration for one Roman soldier per day was one quart of wheat. Here, then, a working man had to feed his whole family, a wife, six, eight, ten children, and himself on one quart of wheat. However, one might buy three quarts of barley which was a less desirable grain because it made a dark black bread. One could, however, survive on barley bread.

In many of the Roman famines the common people starved for

lack of wheat but the rich had plenty of oil and wine and feasted sumptuously every day. This has been true throughout the history of the world. The specter of famine is a shadow falling over the poor of the world, while often the rich eat well and fare well. The problem of famine continues in our modern world and will be so until the end of the age.

Scene 4
The Fourth Seal Vision—The Pale Green Horse (6:7-8)

When he opened the fourth seal, I heard the voice of the fourth living creature say, "Come!" And I saw, and behold a pale horse, and its rider's name was Death and Hades followed him; and they were given power over a fourth of the earth, to kill with sword and with famine and with pestilence and by wild beasts of the earth.

Following conquering, warfare, and famine the fourth horse of death appears on the scene. Its color is pale green. The Greek word is *chloros,* meaning a pale yellow-green—the color of a corpse on the battlefield. Following the horse is Hades, the realm of the dead. Death has always followed conquering, warfare, and famine. Through every major war in history bodies have covered the landscape. Pale green in our color code is the color for death; dark green the color for life.

One fourth of the earth is affected. In the number code fractions represent incompleteness. Death in every age has its incomplete victories on the battlefields of the world. In Hebrew thought Hades was a place under the earth for the dead. In the earliest pages of the Old Testament there was no view of life after death; everyone went to a place called Sheol which was the Hebrew equivalent of Hades. Later the Pharisees developed a concept of life after death. Hades was split with the righteous on one side and the unrighteous on the other; a barrier divided the habitation. The unrighteous could look over the barrier and observe the reward of the righteous. In Christian life the two places were separated. The place for the righteous dead became paradise or heaven; Hades became the dwelling place for the unrighteous dead. In Revelation it symbolizes the place of the dead; it should be seen as a separate place from Gehenna which means hell.

Scene 5
The Fifth Seal Vision—The Martyrs (6:9-11)

When he opened the fifth seal, I saw under the altar the souls of those
who had been slain for the word of God and for the witness they had
borne; they cried out with a loud voice, "O Sovereign Lord, holy and
true, how long before thou wilt judge and avenge our blood on those
who dwell upon the earth?" Then they were each given a white robe
and told to rest a little longer, until the number of their fellow brethren should be complete, who were to be killed as they themselves had
been.

We now see under the altar of sacrifice in heaven the souls of those
who have been slain because of the Word of God and their testimony.
These are the Christian martyrs down through the centuries. In the
midst of conquering, warfare, famine, and death, Christians will also
be called upon to stand firmly for what they believe. To give your
witness meant in the ancient world to stake your life on your beliefs.
The theme in this act has been the altar of sacrifice which stood in
the Jewish Temple before the entrance into the holy of holies. It was
fourteen feet tall with a ramp leading to the top of the altar. An
animal would be taken up there, its throat would be cut and the
blood would be caught and dashed against the foot of the altar.

Instead of the animal's blood on the foot of the altar, John saw the
blood of the martyrs. These martyrs are calling for God to bring his
judgment upon the world and to punish the Romans who have put
them to death. They are told to rest for a little while until their
number is complete. Verse 11 in this passage is very important for
it tells us the truth that down through world history there will be
people who are called upon to give up their lives for the cause of
Christ. We live in strange times in our own country of America
where we have had very few martyrs. However, in parts of the world
where persecution is still going on, *many* Christians have paid the
ultimate price. The day may even come in our own land when to be
a Christian means to stake your life on what you believe. In reading
church history, one soon discovers the great theme of martyrdom
running throughout all the ages. In our own country, we rarely hear
about religious persecution. However, how long will that kind of
situation last? God is telling the martyrs that when the last martyr

has given up his life, then God will judge the world, but not until that time.

The white robes which they are given are symbols of immortality and the immortal body. Throughout world history we have seen this long line of martyrs, men and women who have paid the price so we might worship as we please today.

Scene 6
The Sixth Seal Vision—A Preview of World Judgment (6:12-17)

When he opened the sixth seal, I looked, and behold, there was a great earthquake; and the sun became black as sackcloth, the full moon became like blood, and the stars of the sky fell to the earth as the fig tree sheds its winter fruit when shaken by a gale; the sky vanished like a scroll that is rolled up, and every mountain and island was removed from its place. Then the kings of the earth and the great men and the generals and the rich and the strong, and every one, slave and free, hid in the caves and among the rocks of the mountains, calling to the mountains and rocks, "Fall on us and hide us from the face of him who is seated on the throne, and from the wrath of the Lamb; for the great day of their wrath has come, and who can stand before it?"

The sixth seal is opened and there is a great earthquake and the sun darkens and the moon becomes as red as blood. The stars fall out of the heaven upon the earth as ripe figs and the whole heaven is rolled up as a scroll. This is a preview of world judgment. It does not take place here but later in Act VI. God shows to the martyrs a preview of his judgment. It is proleptic in design. When God does judge the world it will be complete. John uses all the symbolic language of apocalyptic literature, the sun turning black as sackcloth of hair, the moon red as blood, the sky being rolled up as a scroll. The whole universe will be shattered. This gives great hope to the martyrs who are calling out for God to judge the world. It would also have been a great source of strength to the Christian families who heard it. Many of them had lost loved ones in the persecutions of Domitian. Great hope was brought to them that one day God would judge the world.

Interlude: The Sealing of the 144,000 (7:1-17)

After this I saw four angels standing at the four corners of the earth, holding back the four winds of the earth, that no wind might blow on

earth or sea or against any tree. Then I saw another angel ascend from
the rising of the sun, with the seal of the living God, and he called with
a loud voice to the four angels who had been given power to harm
earth and sea, saying, "Do not harm the earth or the sea or the trees,
till we have sealed the servants of our God upon their foreheads." And
I heard the number of the sealed, a hundred and forty-four thousand
sealed, out of every tribe of the sons of Israel.

This hope is further underlined in an interlude in the action in
chapter 7. Interludes are very important in the Book of Revelation.
They are not intermissions as we have in our dramas today but
rather a time for important actions to aid in interpretation. These
interludes take place on the side ledge of the stage. The interlude
here is to seal 144,000 before God's judgment comes upon the face
of the earth. First of all in our number code, 144,000 is based on the
number twelve (12,000 X 12), which stands for wholeness. All the
true believers will be sealed from the judgment of God that will come
upon the earth. John picks up this theme from Exodus 11.

The plagues which will come in Act III of Revelation are very
similar to the ten plagues that came upon Egypt. Before those
plagues came the Jewish people were sealed—especially from the
angel of death. A mark of lamb's blood was put upon the doorpost
to protect the true people of God. In Revelation, John sees a similar
kind of thing. The blood of the Lamb will protect the true believers.
They may have to suffer and be persecuted and even become martyrs, but the judgment of God will not be brought upon them. In
John's theology, judgment is always something which we bring upon
ourselves. He does not portray God throwing thunderbolts down
from heaven in the way some ancient Greek god might do. God
creates us in freedom and allows us to make our choices. If we choose
to go in the way of darkness, God gives us over to that way and we
bring his judgment upon ourselves. True Christian believers thus
would not have God's judgment brought upon them. Chapter 7 then
is a beautiful message of hope for Christians.

There are some sect groups that say only 144,000 people are going
to heaven. Revelation is saying the opposite. They miss the symboli-
cal significance of 144,000; all true believers are sealed.

Angels are told to hold back God's winds of destruction. They do
this until the people of God are sealed upon their forehead with the

sign of the Lamb. John then lists the 144,000 according to the twelve tribes of Israel. One should not be misled at this point to see these as 144,000 Jews. John has left us several clues that we might know that we are dealing with the new Israel or the Christian church. The listing of the tribes of Israel that we see in 7:5-8 is most unique in that the tribe of Judah is listed first. If you were to stop a Jew on the street and ask him to list the twelve tribes of Israel he would not be likely to list Judah first but rather Reuben, the oldest child. By listing Judah first John has given us the indication that we are dealing with the new Israel for the Messiah was to come from that tribe. The tribe of Dan is missing. No Jew would leave out the tribe of Dan in listing the group of twelve. Many early Christians thought that the Antichrist would come from the tribe of Dan.

In addition, throughout the New Testament the theme is that the church is the true Israel of God. You will find that teaching very strong in Romans 9—11. There Paul talks about two olive trees, a cultivated olive tree and a wild olive tree. The cultivated tree represents the Jewish nation and the wild olive tree the Gentile nation. Paul declared that the branches of the Jewish tree were broken out and the Gentile branches were grafted in. Thus today the true tree of Israel is the Christian church. Why did God do that? Paul asked. In order to make the Jews jealous so that one day they might return to the tree of faith. Also in the letters to the churches of Smyrna and Philadelphia, Jews are called a synagogue of Satan (2:9; 3:9) and the Christian church is presented as the true Israel of God. Thus the 144,000 are here the people of God, the true believers in the church throughout all of the centuries, and they are sealed with God's seal of protection.

John reemphasizes the martyr theme in the last part of the chapter (7:9-17). In the first eight verses of chapter 7 we have seen the church militant—the martyrs struggling and fighting. The seal of God is placed upon the true believers down through the ages. In verses 9-17 we see the church triumphant, martyrs down through the centuries marching into heaven singing beautiful hymns as they come before the throne of God. They are waving palm branches and singing:

Salvation belongs to our God who sits upon the throne and to the
Lamb! (7:10).

And all the angels of heaven join in singing:

Amen! Blessing and glory and wisdom and thanksgiving and honor
and power and might be to our God for ever and ever! Amen (7:12).

Then the martyrs continue to sing:

Therefore they are before the throne of God,/and serve him day and
night within his temple;/and he who sits upon the throne will shelter
them with his presence./They shall hunger no more, neither thirst
any more;/the sun shall not strike them, nor any scorching heat./For
the Lamb in the midst of the throne will be their shepherd,/and he will
guide them to springs of living water;/and God shall wipe every tear
from their eyes (7:15-17).

Scene 7
The Seventh Seal Vision—The Golden Incense Containers (8:1-4)

When the Lamb opened the seventh seal, there was silence in heaven
for about half an hour. Then I saw the seven angels who stand before
God, and seven trumpets were given to them. And another angel came
and stood at the altar with a golden censer; and he was given much
incense to mingle with the prayers of all the saints upon the golden
altar before the throne; and the smoke of the incense rose with the
prayers of the saints from the hand of the angel before God.

Following this interlude of the sealing of the 144,000 the seventh
seal is broken open. There is silence in heaven for half an hour. This
is to punctuate the importance of the next part of the act. Seven
angels come out on the stage, and seven trumpets are given to them.
The seventh scene in each act leads us into the stage setting for the
next act. Another angel came and stood at the incense altar and
much incense was given to him to mix with the prayers of God's
people. This is a beautiful message of hope for the Christians who are
being persecuted. In the midst of their persecution God's hand rests
upon them. They have been sealed. Also their prayers are heard
daily as they are mixed with the incense coming up before the throne
of God. Then the incense containers are filled with hot coals and
thrown down upon the face of the earth. There is thundering and
lightning and a great earthquake ending Act II.

Act II has shown us the scope of world history, conquering, warfare, famine, and death. In the midst of these forces Christians have to take their stand, and some will die for the cause of Christ. Yet, in the midst of this is a great message of hope that God one day will judge the world. In the meantime true believers are sealed and their prayers are heard daily before the throne of God. This message was very important to Christians in the first century who were facing death for Christ. In a timeless sense, it is a message that has been important to every Christian down through world history. In times of severe persecution, Christians have always turned to Revelation because of its message of hope.

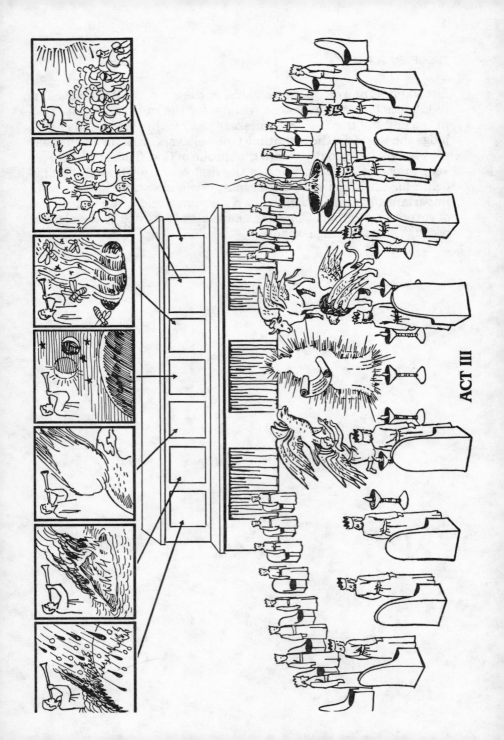

ACT III

Act III
The Seven Trumpets

Revelation 8:5 to 11:18

Stage Setting

Seven angels come out of the Temple on the lower stage and ascend the ramp leading up to the ledge (*proskene*). The angels stand in front of the seven windows (*thuromata*). As each angel blows his trumpet, he walks to the ledge overlooking the chorus. The seven plagues which this act will bring are pictured in the seven windows behind the angels. These are very similar to the Egyptian plagues outlined in the Book of Exodus

1. Plague on the Nile
2. Plague of frogs
3. Plague of gnats
4. Plague of flies
5. Plague of cattle
6. Plague of boils
7. Plague of hail
8. Plague of locusts
9. Plague of darkness
10. Plague on the firstborn

In this act the number one third is emphasized. In the number code fractions represent incompleteness; this is God's incomplete judgment upon the world. The whole purpose of the act is to show God's mercy, with the plagues intended to bring about repentance from sinful mankind. In every age, if we have eyes of faith, we can see God's hand of judgment upon the world. It is not a picture of God throwing thunderbolts down from Mount Olympus; rather John sets forth in his theology that we bring God's judgment upon ourselves. God created us with freedom and allows us to exercise our own self-will. If we choose the way of darkness, then we also choose the way of judgment. John depicts in symbolic terms all of nature revolt-

63

ing against the sin of mankind. Signs in heaven and on earth portray the enormity of the earth's reaction toward the conduct of man. The whole earth is pictured as being in turmoil in the grip of divine judgment.

Gibbon, in his book *The Decline and Fall of the Roman Empire,* lists three reasons for the fall of Rome: natural calamities, the inner rot and decay of society, and the invasion of the barbarians. The first four trumpets of Act III deal with this first reason, natural calamities. Trumpet 5 depicts the inner rot and decay of Rome as monster beasts, monster locusts coming up from a pit. Trumpet 6 sets forth the third reason for Rome's fall as the invasion of the barbarians, two hundred million horsemen, cross the Euphrates to march on Rome.

The Jewish Temple

In the background of the lower stage stands the altar of incense. Earlier the angels had taken hot coals from this altar and thrown them out upon the face of the earth. As the trumpets sound from the upper stage, this altar glows in the background, symbolizing the judgment of God. In Act I, John emphasized the seven branch candlestick in the holy place. In Act II the spotlight fell upon the altar of sacrifice. Each act of Revelation will emphasize some theme from the Jewish Temple.

The Chorus

The chorus of the twenty-four elders remains on the lower stage to sing the music of Revelation. God sits on his throne, surrounded by the four living creatures; a dark green rainbow stands over the throne. Seven burning torches flare before the throne and the whole chorus level is separated from the audience by a sea of glass.

Scene 1
The First Trumpet—Plague of Hail, Fire, Blood (8:7)

The first angel blew his trumpet, and there followed hail and fire, mixed with blood, which fell on the earth; and a third of the earth was burnt up and third of the trees were burnt up, and all the grass was burnt up.

These words bring to mind the seventh plague of Egypt (Ex. 9:24) except here the fear has been heightened by the addition of blood. This plague falls upon one third of the trees with one third of the earth burned up. There is a Jewish midrash on Psalm 2:9 which reads, "A third of all the world's woes will come in the day of the Messiah." In John's day and time the people had witnessed the red sand blowing in from the Sahara Desert which, mixed with the rainfall, would appear like red flames in the air. Yet John is seeing something even greater than that. God's world is rebelling against the sins of mankind. Throughout the Bible, emphasis is placed upon the fact that there is a relationship between man's environment and himself. In Romans 8 we are told that the whole world is yearning for redemption; man's sin has spilled over on all the universe; the world will rebel against man's sin. In the cyclical sense of the plague we might well look at our own world today. We have been given this earth to care for; Genesis teaches that man is to have dominion over the world but this does not give us the excuse to abuse it.

When our forefathers first came to the shores of America, there were trees reaching from the east coast to the west coast. Over the years we have wasted our natural resources. In the newspapers we read of acid rain, moving from the midwest to the northeast, destroying the greenery and fresh water lakes of our land. It is not so hard, then, to understand the eternal message of this Act of Revelation. Man is related to his world, and we bring judgment upon ourselves when we abuse our world. The commercial shown on television in which an Indian stands with a great big tear in his eye looking out at a devastated and polluted national forest illustrates that truth. Yet the one-third destruction symbolizes the mercy of God; there is time to repent before it is too late. The modern world is becoming much more concerned about the welfare and upkeep of the environment.

Scene 2
The Second Trumpet—Plague on the Sea (8:8-9)

The second angel blew his trumpet, and something like a great mountain, burning with fire, was thrown into the sea; and a third of the sea became blood, a third of the living creatures in the sea died, and a third of the ships were destroyed.

The plague on the sea is very similar to the first Egyptian plague on the Nile River; both bodies of water become blood. Again, many natural phenomena of that period of time resemble the effect here. In the volcanic eruption at Santorini, Roman scholars tell us the sea turned red from the molten lava hitting the water. In the Sibylline Oracles (5:58-61) we find a verse: "A great star will fall into the sea and destroy it, along with Babylon (Rome) for oppressing of the Jews." Blood symbolized pollution in the Jewish religion. A sea turning into blood would be a sign of pollution; one third of the sea creatures were destroyed.

In a timeless sense we see this message clearly in our own day. Again, we have not managed our world very well. At the end of World War II canisters of nerve gas were brought by train from the interior of the United States and thrown into the Atlantic Ocean. If one of these cannisters were to come open, much of the life in the sea would be destroyed. It is not difficult to understand the judgment we have brought upon ourselves in these circumstances by careless pollution of the seas.

Scene 3
The Third Trumpet—Plague on the Fresh Water (8:10-11)

The third angel blew his trumpet, and a great star fell from heaven, blazing like a torch, and fell on a third of the rivers and on the fountains of water. The name of the star is Wormwood. A third of the water became wormwood, and many men died of the water, because it was made bitter.

This plague is upon the fresh water of the world. Wormwood was not considered a poisonous herb, but it did have a bitter taste (Prov. 5:4). Many Jews believed that in the last days all the stars would fall. In Jeremiah 9:15 we read, "Therefore thus says the Lord of hosts, the God of Israel: Behold, I will feed this people with wormwood, and give them poisonous water to drink." John probably had in mind a burning volcano with lava hitting a cold stream of water. Vesuvius had erupted in August of AD 79, yet John's picture is of something even more devastating than that.

In our own day we again realize the timeless truth of the cyclical view of Revelation. Again we have mismanaged our world, especially our streams of water. Many of you reading this book are aware of the pollution of our nation's streams and rivers, perhaps in your own town. It is not hard for us to see the relationship between the earth and mankind. John is emphasizing the truth that the earth is rebelling against the sin of man. Ecology teaches us about this relationship. Even though John may not have had this in mind specifically when he wrote Revelation, the timeless message becomes real for us today.

Scene 4
The Fourth Trumpet—Plague on the Heavenly Bodies (8:12)

The fourth angel blew his trumpet, and a third of the sun was struck, and a third of the moon, and a third of the stars, so that a third of their light was darkened; a third of the day was kept from shining, and likewise a third of the night.

This plague corresponds in many ways to the ninth Egyptian plague of darkness (Ex. 10:21-23). People living in and around Mount Vesuvius had experienced many of these signs in AD 79. The volcanic ash had darkened the skies and many thought the heavenly bodies had lost their light. It is not hard for John's readers to visualize this happening again, demonstrating the rebellion of the world against the sin of man.

In the timeless sequence, we today are very much aware of our relationship to the heavenly bodies. In an era where the garbage of space might rain down upon us at any moment, it is not hard for us to understand. Scientists tell us that by using certain brands of hairspray, we are depleting the ozone layer in the heavens, causing an increase in skin cancer. Man is related directly to his environment. John's timeless truths are evident in every age.

Interlude (8:13)

Then I looked, and I heard an eagle crying with a loud voice, as it flew in midheaven, "Woe, woe, woe to those who dwell on earth, at the blasts of the other trumpets which the three angels are about to blow."

In an interlude in the action, an eagle flies across the heavens. In our animal code the eagle represents the bearer of bad news. Even when the eagle is not present, John uses the cry of the eagle, in Greek, *ouai*. When the word is pronounced quickly, the sound is that of an eagle's screeching. Greeks loved to use such words which mimicked the sound of the particular animal. The next three trumpets are called *ouais* or woes. They are far worse than the previous trumpets. The eagle was considered to be an unclean bird of prey by Jews, and it was ranked together in the general classification of vulture. In the Old Testament the eagle or vulture is often the symbol for an invading army (Deut. 28:49; Jer. 48:40; Hab. 1:8).

Scene 5
The Fifth Trumpet—Plague of the Locusts (9:1-12)

And the fifth angel blew his trumpet, and I saw a star fallen from heaven to earth, and he was given the key of the shaft of the bottomless pit; he opened the shaft of the bottomless pit, and from the shaft rose smoke like the smoke of a great furnace, and the sun and the air were darkened with the smoke from the shaft. Then from the smoke came locusts on the earth, and they were given power like the power of the scorpions of the earth; they were told not to harm the grass of the earth or any green growth or any tree, but only those of mankind who have not the seal of God upon their forehead; they were allowed to torture them for five months, but not to kill them, and their torture was like the torture of a scorpion when it stings a man. And in those days men will seek death and will not find it; they will long to die, and death will fly from them. In appearance the locusts were like horses arrayed for battle; on their heads were what looked like crowns of gold; their faces were like human faces, their hair like women's hair, and their teeth like lion's teeth; they had scales like iron breast plates, and the noise of their wings was like the noise of many chariots with horses rushing into battle. They have tails like scorpions, and stings, and their power of hurting men for five months lies in their tails. They have as king over them the angel of the bottomless pit; his name in Hebrew is Abaddon, and in Greek he is called Apollyon. The first woe has passed; behold, two woes are still to come.

The locusts from the pit are our first monster beasts in the Book of Revelation. Monster beasts represent monstrous persons or forces. Everything about the description of these beasts would point to their vile nature. They are not really locusts; they are the size of horses; their faces are human and their hair, women's hair and their teeth, lion's teeth. They have stingers in their tails like scorpions. John has put together some of the most frightening aspects of the world of nature and molded one gigantic monster beast. The Hebrew world felt that volcanos led into the interior of the earth. Some believed that in the so-called abyss dwelt demons, fallen angels, and other evil spirits. Many believed that the fallen angels of Genesis 6 were incarcerated in that place. John's vision has the monster locusts coming up out of the bottomless pit and bringing their scourge across the earth for five months. In the number code, five represents penalty or punishment.

The locusts here represent the inner rot and decay of Rome. If you were to select one animal to represent the ugliness of sin in our own society, what animal would you select? There is really no animal mean enough to represent sin. John, therefore, constructed a monster beast to represent a monstrous force. We have already said that Gibbon in his book listed as one of the three reasons for the fall of Rome the decadence of that society. When the barbarians got to the gates of Rome, they did not have to fight. The city was so corrupt on the inside that it capitulated. If you have eyes of faith, you can see the monster beast at work in our own society. Some interpreters worry about who these beasts will be twenty or thirty years from now. Grotesque pictures are portrayed of helicopters and other modern instruments of warfare. That attitude overlooks the beasts that are working now in the very foundations of our own society. We see them at work in the abuse of drugs, the increase of pornography, the rising rate of crime, and the threat of nuclear warfare. If we keep our eyes only on the future, we will not be genuinely concerned about dealing with the monster beasts at work in our own society. John has rightly portrayed this force of evil and sin in our world as a monster beast, ugly and despicable. Every age has to deal with the impact of these locusts that are working for evil in our world. Five months is a symbolic number for punishment. In addition, the locust infestations in Israel usually occurred in the last five months of the Jewish calendar.

The ruler over the bottomless pit is called Abaddon or Apollyon. Abaddon is somewhat similar to Belial as mentioned in the Dead Sea Scrolls. There he is a military leader of Israel and is the champion of the forces of darkness which are allowed to be unleashed against Israel so that he might spread his dominion of evil over the world. On Yahweh's day of judgment the angels of righteousness will destroy all the enemies of Israel, led by Belial. The Greek god Apollo at his chief temple at Delphi was symbolized by grasshoppers or locusts; he also used the bow and arrow to poison his enemies. Thus both Greek and Hebrew background are brought together in the figure of the angel guarding the bottomless pit.

Scene 6
The Sixth Trumpet—Plague of 200 Million Horsemen (9:13-21)

Then the sixth angel blew his trumpet, and I heard a voice from the four horns of the golden altar before God, saying to the sixth angel who had the trumpet, "Release the four angels who are bound in the great river Euphrates." So the four angels were released, who had been held ready for the hour, the day, the month, and the year, to kill a third of mankind. The number of the troops of cavalry was twice ten thousand times ten thousand; I heard their number. And this was how I saw the horses in my vision; the riders wore breastplates the color of fire and of sapphire and of sulfur, and the heads of the horses were like lions' heads, and smoke and fire and sulfur issued from their mouths. By these three plagues a third of mankind was killed, by the fire and smoke and sulfur issuing from their mouths. For the power of the horses is in their mouths and in their tails; the tails are like serpents, with heads, and by means of them they wound. The rest of mankind, who were not killed by these plagues, did not repent of the works of their hands or give up worshiping demons and idols of gold and silver and bronze and stone and wood, which cannot either see or hear or walk; nor did they repent of their murders or sorceries or their immorality or their thefts.

The sixth plague brings the invasion of the barbarians, a demonic monster horde gathered at the Euphrates River. The Euphrates marked the eastern boundary of the Roman Empire. Beyond that river the Parthians ruled. The Romans were never able to subdue the Parthians and they were considered the most barbaric people of that day. Eventually Rome would fall to the barbarians from the East. Gibbon lists as the third reason for the fall of Rome the invasion of the barbarians. The horses are not normal horses, nor are the riders normal warriors. The breastplates are made of fire, sapphire, and sulfur. The Parthian army used armor made of metal which often rusted and became fiery red in color. The heads of the horses are like lion's heads with fire, smoke, and brimstone coming from their mouths. Their tails are like snakes, injuring mankind. What better symbols to represent the barbaric forces throughout world history?

In the Old Testament we find the Northern Kingdom is warned by

Amos, Hosea, and other prophets to repent before it is too late. The Israelites did not listen and the Assyrian nation marched upon Samaria in 722 BC and brought destruction upon the land. The ten northern tribes were marched into captivity, fishhooks through their lips, and no one to this day knows what really happened to them. Foreigners were brought in and settled in old Samaria and became the Samaritan people of the New Testament time. The Southern Kingdom did not learn from history when the prophets such as Jeremiah warned them. Many Israelites believed that nothing could happen to Judea because of the presence of God's Temple. God would not allow one stone to be disturbed in that majestic building. Yet in 587 BC the Babylonians marched upon Jerusalem, took the young and the rich into captivity to the great city of Babylon. In turning their backs upon God the Jewish people had brought God's judgment upon themselves through the barbarians.

Throughout history we can see the cyclical chain of events, barbarians marching across the face of the earth. There are many in our own country who make the mistake of equating America with Israel. Ancient Israel was a nation ruled by priests and governed by the Sanhedrin. Although we cannot equate the two countries, we can hear the basic message of this part of Revelation. No nation is ever so godly or ever so pious that it is immune from the forces and tides of world history. Some Americans believe that nothing can happen to America because it is a godly nation. Yet the cyclical pattern of Revelation shows the pattern of barbarians emerging in every age. Hitler boasted of Nazism lasting a thousand years and it barely made it to ten years. Nations opposed to God bring his judgment upon them.

The plague of barbarians is set loose by four angels who are chained at the Euphrates River. They are released to bring destruction upon mankind. In 1 Enoch 56:5 we read, "In those days the angels shall hurl themselves to the east upon the Parthians and Meades."

Interlude (10:1 to 11:14)

The interlude may be divided into three subscenes: John eats the scroll, measures the Temple, two witnesses appear.

John Eats a Scroll (10:1-11)

Then I saw another mighty angel coming down from heaven, wrapped in a cloud, with a rainbow over his head and his face was like the sun, and his legs like pillars of fire. He had a little scroll open in his hand. And he set his right foot on the sea, and his left foot on the land, and called out with a loud voice, like a lion roaring; When he called out, the seven thunders sounded. And when the seven thunders had sounded, I was about to write, but I heard a voice from heaven saying, "Seal up what the seven thunders have said; do not write it down." And the angel whom I saw standing upon the sea and land lifted up his right hand to heaven and swore by him who lives forever and ever, who created heaven and what is in it, the earth and what is in it, and the sea and what is in it, so there should be no more delay, but that in the days of the trumpet call to be sounded by the seventh angel, the mystery of God as he announced to his servants the prophets, should be fulfilled. Then the voice which I heard from heaven spoke to me again saying, "Go, take the scroll which is open in the hands of the angel who is standing on the sea and on the land." So I went to the angel and told him to give me the little scroll; and he said to me, "Take it and eat; it will be bitter to your stomach but sweet as honey in your mouth." And I took the little scroll from the hand of the angel and ate it; it was sweet as honey in my mouth, but when I had eaten it my stomach was made bitter. I was told, "You must again prophesy about many peoples and nations and tongues and kings."

Here we find a description of the strong or mighty angel coming down from heaven to present John with a little scroll. There are two important scrolls in the Book of Revelation. The first scroll mentioned is found in the hands of God in chapter 4. That scroll contained the revelations found in chapters 1 through 9. The present scroll which the angel holds contains the final chapters of the Book of Revelation. The angel might well be the angel Gabriel since his name meant *strong* in Hebrew. The rainbow over his head is the reflection of his face upon the cloud.

John starts to write down the voices of the seven thunders which he hears; this would have been an eighth act in Revelation. However, he is forbidden to write down the contents of this act and told to seal it up. Its message was not to be heard. Verses 5 through 7 point to the power and might of the Creator God and declare that there shall be no more delay when the trumpet introduces the last acts of Revelation and the final movement of God in the world. In verses 8-11 John is told to take the little scroll and eat it. To eat here symbolizes the reading and digesting of the contents of the scroll. John found it sweet in his mouth but bitter in his stomach.

When he first read the message that the Roman Empire would be defeated, and God would reign, this brought joy and sweetness to his life. However, when he saw the horrors of the last days, it became bitter in his mouth. We are reminded of the story of Ezekiel found in 2:8f, when Ezekiel is told to swallow a small book with woes against ancient Israel. To Ezekiel it is sweet in his mouth, but there is no mention of its being bitter in his stomach. However, the contents of the book did bring woe. In Jeremiah 15:16-17 we find the message:

> Thy words were found, and I ate them,
>   and thy words became to me a joy
>   and the delight of my heart;
> for I am called by thy name,
>   O Lord, God of Hosts.

Measuring the Temple (11:1-2)

> Then I was given a measuring rod like a staff, and I was told: "Rise and measure the temple of God and the altar and those that worship there, but do not measure the court outside the temple; leave that out, for it is given over to the nations, and they will trample over the holy city for forty-two months."

During the interlude another message of security is given to the believers. In chapter 7 they had been sealed upon their forehead. Here in chapter 11 they are measured. The Jewish Temple consisted of several interlocking courts, starting with the court of the Gentiles, and proceeding to the court of the women, to the court of Israel, to the court of the priests, and finally to the holy of holies. The inner courts for Jews only were called the *Naos*. The outer courts of the Temple, along with the Jewish part, were called the *Hieron*. John is told to measure only the inner Jewish part of the Temple. Again John is using the theme of the new Israel, the church; all true Christians are measured or protected against the woes to come. The outer court, the court of the Gentiles, represents all unbelievers; it will be trampled down for an incomplete period of time, three and a half years. John also liked to use the equivalent number, 42 months or 1,260 days; this is his way of showing and intensifying an incomplete period of time. This is another wonderful message for believers, all true believers will be measured and protected, even as they have been sealed.

Appearance of the Two Witnesses (11:3-14)

And I will grant my two witnesses power to prophesy for one thousand two hundred and sixty days, clothed in sackcloth. These are the two olive trees and two lampstands which stand before the Lord of the earth. And if any one would harm them, fire pours from their mouth and consumes their foes; if any one would harm them, thus he is doomed to be killed. They have power to shut the sky, that no rain may fall during the days of their prophesying, and they have power over the waters to turn them into blood, and to smite the earth with every plague, as often as they desire. And when they have finished their testimony, the beast that ascends from the bottomless pit will make war upon them, and conquer them and kill them, and their dead bodies will lie in the street of the great city which is allegorically called Sodom and Egypt, where their Lord was crucified. For three days and a half men from the peoples and tribes and tongues and nations gaze at their dead bodies and refuse to let them be placed in a tomb, and those who dwell on the earth will rejoice over them and make merry and exchange presents, because these two prophets have been a torment to those who dwell on the earth. But after the three and a half days a breath of life from God entered them, and they stood up on their feet, and great fear fell on those who saw them. Then they heard a loud voice from heaven saying to them, "Come up hither!" And in the sight of their foes, they went up to heaven in a cloud. And at that hour there was a great earthquake, and a tenth of the city fell; seven thousand people were killed in the earthquake, and the rest were terrified and gave glory to the God of heaven. The second woe has passed; behold, the third woe is soon to come.

In verse 3 there has been much debate about the identity of the two witnesses. From the description given to us in verses 5 and 6 we can conclude that they are quite likely Moses and Elijah. Some believe that perhaps they are Enoch and Elijah; however, it seems that Moses and Elijah would fit the text much better. These witnesses have the power to turn water into blood and to bring plagues upon the earth; this would remind us very much of Moses and the first Egyptian plague (Ex. 7:14). They also have power to consume with fire and to close up the heaven so it should rain no more on the earth. This would remind us of Elijah in 2 Kings 1:10. Many Jews

also believed that both men, Moses and Elijah, had been taken
straight to heaven and would return before the end of the age. In the
transfiguration of Christ one also encounters Moses and Elijah. In
verse 4 our text rests heavily upon Zachariah 4:2-3,14, yet differs in
many points. In Zachariah there is one candlestick with seven lamps
which are said to be the eyes of the Lord going to and fro throughout
the whole earth. Beside the candlestick there are two olive trees
which are said to be Joshua and Zerubbabel. Here in Revelation the
one candlestick has been changed to two. The two candlesticks and
the two olive trees are synonymous. Hence, Moses and Elijah are the
two candlesticks and they bring the divine light of God which one
finds in the law and in the prophecy.

In verses 7-10 a beast rises up against the two witnesses and puts
them to death and their bodies lie in the city streets of Sodom and
Egypt. For three and a half days people celebrate over the death of
the two witnesses. In verses 7-13 the two witnesses are brought back
to life and taken up to heaven while a great earthquake falls upon
the city.

This interlude speaks to us of an actual happening in the ancient
world. For the Jewish people the *Bible* was always symbolized by
Moses and Elijah. In the synagogue a passage was read from the
prophets and a passage from the law. In many of the seven churches
of Asia Minor, the Word of God had been taken from the Christian
people, sometimes burned in the city square. The two witnesses
represent the Word of God. The death of the two witnesses represents the attempt of the Roman government to destroy the Word of
God by burning the Scriptures and destroying them. The beast coming up out of the pit would be the Roman Empire. The people in the
city celebrate the destruction of God's Word. At the very moment
when the Romans feel they have won the battle, two witnesses appear once again. There is a message of hope here for true believers.
God's Word will never be destroyed; it will be an aid and guide to the
Christian martyrs as they confront the Roman army.

In Act II the believers had received the assurance that they were
sealed on their foreheads and their prayers were heard before the
throne of God. In Act III the believers receive the promise that they
will be measured and God's Word will be with them even in the
darkest days of persecution. The three and a half days will be an

incomplete time of persecution. The seven thousand might well represent the city of Jerusalem symbolizing the people of God.

Scene 7
The Seventh Trumpet—Worship of the 24 Elders (11:15-18)

Then the seventh angel blew his trumpet, and there were loud voices in heaven saying, "The kingdom of the world has become the kingdom of our Lord and of his Christ, and he shall reign for ever and ever." And the twenty-four elders who sit on their thrones before God fell on their faces and worshiped God, saying,
"We give thanks to thee, Lord God Almighty, who art and who wast,
    that thou hast taken thy great power and begun to reign.
The nations raged, but thy wrath came,
    and the time for the dead to be judged,
for rewarding thy servants, the prophets and saints,
    and those who fear thy name, both small and great
and for destroying the destroyers of the earth."

Act III concludes with worship in heaven. The choir of twenty-four elders sings of God's complete victory even though that event has not yet happened in Revelation. In fact their hymn in verses 17-18 contains an outline of the last four acts of Revelation. In these acts we will read about the uprising of the nations against the rule of God. Even in the midst of that conflict, God's rule is assured. While the choir is singing, the curtains leading into the holy of holies of the Jewish Temple are parted and we behold the ark of the covenant. This act is a symbol of God's constancy; his promises continue through world history.

The choir also sings of the last things in world history—judgment and the resurrection of the dead. The cyclical movement in Revelation is combined with a linear time concept. A special effect is produced. Even as certain cycles are repeated, time is moving forward. The choir looks across that line of history and sings of those last time events as if they were now happening.

Act III has shown us God's hand of judgment at work within history. The whole world rebels against the sin of man. John did not paint a picture in this act of an angry God raining judgment down upon earth and man. Rather, human beings bring God's judgment upon themselves. God creates us in freedom and allows us to make our own choices. If we choose the way of darkness, we bring this judgment upon ourselves. In a symbolic sense, the whole earth rebels against us. Sin has influenced our whole environment.

Rome fell as Gibbon tells us because of natural calamities, inner rot and decay, and the invasion of the barbarians. It is obvious that John was depicting Rome and its moral sickness in Act III. Yet the Act has a cyclical timeless message. In every age, we will find the same evil forces at work in the world. The monster locusts (inner rot and decay) prowl across the earth. Human societies rise and fall. The barbarians of the world are always on the move. Man's fate is related to his environment. More than any other age, we see the results of an abused environment, and our children may reap the awful harvest.

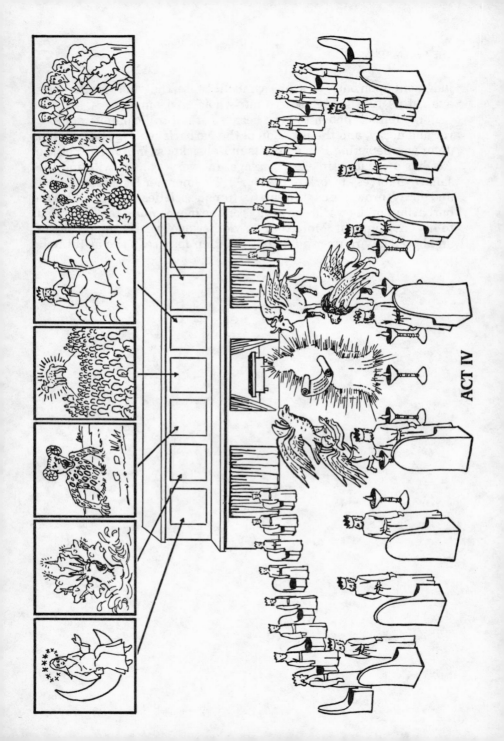

ACT IV

Act IV
The Seven Tableaux

Revelation 11:19 to 15:4

Stage Setting

The throne room of God continues to be the setting on the main stage or chorus level. Behind the throne of God stands a door leading into the Temple. The curtain is open, and we may peer into the holy of holies. There we see the ark of the covenant guarded by 2 cherubim. In the 7 windows of the stage building are 7 tableaux depicting the struggle between good and evil down through world history. The 24 elders are still on the main stage surrounding the throne of God and preparing to sing the hymns of Act IV.

A tableau is a short dramatic piece with two or three main actors. The first 3 tableaux will depict the side of evil, Satan and his 2 helpers portrayed as monster beasts. The next 3 tableaux will show the side of the righteous with the Lamb as the leader. The final tableau will celebrate the victory of the Lamb in hymnic form.

The Jewish Temple

In Act IV the theme from the Temple is the ark of the covenant. In our 3 previous acts we have had the spotlight falling on the seven-branch candlestick, the altar of sacrifice and the altar of incense. The ark of the covenant symbolizes here the promises of God. In the ongoing struggle between good and evil, God's promises are with his people.

Scene 1
The First Tableau—Woman, Child, Dragon (12:1-17)

And a great portent appeared in heaven, a woman clothed with the sun, with the moon under her feet, and on her head a crown of twelve stars; she was with child and she cried out in her pangs of birth, in anguish for delivery. And another portent appeared in heaven; behold a great red dragon, with seven heads and ten horns, and seven diadems upon his heads. His tail swept down a third of the stars of heaven, and cast them to the earth. And the dragon stood before the woman who was about to bear a child, that he might devour her child when she brought it forth; she brought forth a male child, one who is to rule all the nations with a rod of iron, but her child was caught up to God and to his throne, and the woman fled into the wilderness, where she has a place prepared by God, in which to be nourished for one thousand two hundred and sixty days.

Now war arose in heaven, Michael and his angels fighting against the dragon; and the dragon and his angels fought, but they were defeated and there was no longer any place for them in heaven. And the great dragon was thrown down, that ancient serpent, who is called the Devil and Satan, the deceiver of the whole world—he was thrown down to the earth, and his angels were thrown down with him. And I heard a loud voice in heaven, saying, "Now the salvation and the power and the kingdom of our God and the authority of his Christ have come, for the accuser of our brethren has been thrown down, who accuses them day and night before our God. And they have conquered him by the blood of the Lamb and by the word of their testimony, for they loved not their lives even unto death. Rejoice then, O heaven and you that dwell therein! But woe to you, O earth and sea, for the devil has come down to you in great wrath, because he knows that his time is short!"

And when the dragon saw that he had been thrown down to the earth, he pursued the woman who had borne the male child. But the woman was given the two wings of the great eagle that she might fly from the serpent into the wilderness, to the place where she is to be nourished for a time, and times, and half a time. The serpent poured water like a river out of his mouth after the woman, to sweep her away with the flood. But the earth came to the help of the woman, and the earth opened its mouth and swallowed the river which the dragon had poured from his mouth. Then the dragon was angry with the woman, and went off to make war on the rest of her offspring, on those who keep the commandments of God and bear testimony to Jesus. And he stood on the sand of the sea.

In the first tableau, a revolving-door structure called an *eccyclema* is placed in the first window of the stage building. In Greek tragic drama, three such scenes could be placed on this device and turned quickly to depict a more complicated scene. Here in Act IV of Revelation, the first scene has three subscenes: the woman, child, and dragon (12:1-4); the baby is born and taken to heaven (12:5-6); Satan storms heaven and is thrown back to earth where he wars against the woman (12:7-17).

In verses 1-6 we meet the three characters of the first tableau, the woman, the child, and the dragon. The woman is obviously mother Israel, and John has left us several clues to her identity. She stands upon the moon; the Jewish people used a calendar calculated on the basis of the moon. Every 5 years 1 extra month had to be added to the calendar; all the major Jewish festivals were based upon the moon calendar; there were even moon-watching stations across the land so that notice could be sent to Jerusalem when the new moon appeared. The woman also has 12 stars upon her head, representing the 12 tribes of Israel. In 12:2, we are told that she is with child, representing the promise of the Messiah.

The red dragon stands for Satan. John selected a very appropriate symbol for Satan, a sea dragon, since the Jewish people feared the ocean. When they first came to the Promised Land they settled on the mountains because the Philistines were inhabiting the area by the sea. Even to this day, the Jewish nation has never developed a strong navy. They believed that great sea serpents like Leviathan and Behemoth inhabited the outer reaches of the sea. This sea serpent is red in color, symbolizing warfare. His seven heads point to the fact that he desires to be divine or God. Seven crowns denote his attempt to rule this age. The red dragon intends to destroy the child as soon as it is born. Here we see the beginning stages of the great struggle between good and evil.

The child is caught up into heaven and the woman flees into the wilderness where she is kept safe for three and one-half years or 1,260 days. John makes no attempt to give us the life of Jesus; he is born, lives, dies on the cross, and is caught up to heaven in a few seconds. John does want us to see the victory of Jesus Christ over Satan on earth and in heaven and to know that the church is kept safe through all of the difficulty. The woman flees into the desert. During the fall of Jerusalem in AD 70 the Jewish-Christian church fled to a place in the desert, Pella, near the Jordan River. There it remained safe until the Jewish war was over.

In 12:7-12 Satan now storms heaven and is defeated there by Michael and the angels. Michael is viewed as the patron angel of Israel, as the guardian of the righteous of all nations (Dan. 10:13,21). In 1 Enoch 25, Michael is called the patron angel of all the saints in

Israel. Satan is then thrown back to the earth. The chorus sings at this point.

> Now the salvation and the power and the kingdom of God and the authority of his Christ have come, for the accuser of our brethren has been thrown down, who accuses them day and night before our God. And they have conquered him by the blood of the Lamb and by the word of their testimony, for they loved not their lives even unto death. Rejoice then, O heaven and you that dwell therein! But woe to you, O earth and sea, for the devil has come down to you in great wrath, because he knows his time is short! (Rev. 12:10-12).

In the final action in pageant 1 (12:13-17) we now see the dragon turning his attention against the woman and her descendants. Once again it is stated that the woman is kept safe in the desert. The serpent tries to destroy her by pouring forth water from his mouth, but the earth saves the woman by swallowing the water. John tells us very pointedly in verse 17, "Then the dragon was angry with the woman, and went off to make war on the rest of her offspring, on those who keep the commandments of God and bear testimony to Jesus." Here we are caught up into the action and can see the cyclical sense that comes so often in the Book of Revelation. In every age the struggle between good and evil will go on, Satan trying to destroy the righteous and those who bear testimony to Jesus. In the next two tableaux we will see how Satan uses his power to try to control the world in every age.

Scene 2
The Second Tableau—The Beast from the Sea (13:1-10)

And I saw a beast rising out of the sea, with ten horns and seven heads, with ten diadems upon its horns and a blasphemous name upon its heads. And the beast that I saw was like a leopard, its feet were like a bear's, and its mouth was like a lion's mouth. And to it the dragon gave his power and his throne and great authority. One of its heads seemed to have a mortal wound, but its mortal wound was healed, and the whole earth followed the beast with wonder. Men worshiped the dragon, for he had given his authority to the beast, and they worshiped the beast, saying, "Who is like the beast, and who can fight against it?" And the beast was given a mouth uttering haughty and blasphemous words, and it was allowed to exercise authority for forty-two months; it opened its mouth to utter blasphemies against God, blaspheming his name and his dwelling, that is, those who dwell in heaven. Also it was

allowed to make war on the saints and to conquer them. And authority
was given it over every tribe and people and tongue and nation, and
all who dwell on earth will worship it, every one whose name has not
been written before the foundation of the world in the book of life of
the Lamb that was slain. If any one has an ear, let him hear:
If any one is to be taken captive,
to captivity he goes;
if any one slays with the sword,
with the sword must he be slain.
Here is a call for the endurance and faith of the saints.

If you were Satan and wanted to control the world, what would be
the best way to do it? Evil realizes that its best source of power is in
government or political action. John brings together the symbols of
the major world kingdoms of his day and portrays a monstrous
political beast. In 13:1-5 we have a description of this beast. Since
Rome was a major sea power, the beast is depicted as coming forth
from the sea. It is composed of the three symbols of the major powers
of John's day. The bear's feet represent Medea; the leopard's spots,
Persia; the lion's head or mouth, Rome. If John were trying to bring
together a similar composite political beast from our day, he might
use the English bulldog, the Russian bear, and the American eagle.
This horrible beast has seven heads representing the seven Caesars
from the time of the death of Jesus Christ to the time of the Book
of Revelation.

Tiberius	AD 14-37
Caligula	AD 37-41
Claudius	AD 41-54
Nero	AD 54-68
Vespasian	AD 69-79
Titus	AD 79-81
Domitian	AD 81-96

During an eighteen-month period in AD 68-69, three men reigned
who were not always counted in the list of emperors: Galba, Otho,
and Vitellius. The 10 horns also mentioned in the description of the
beast could be these three plus the major seven Caesars.

The mortal wound referred to in verse 3 points to the myth that
had come into being concerning Caesar Nero. Many believed that he
was not really dead and would come back again to rule over the

Roman Empire. Some even believed that Domitian was Nero rein-
carnated. In the last days of Nero's rule, many of his closest friends
had tried to murder him but were unsuccessful. The authority of
Satan is given to this beast from the sea and everyone falls down and
worships before the beast, proclaiming, "Who is like the beast, and
who can fight against it?" (v. 4).

We are told in 13:5-10 of the activity of this beast. The haughty and
blasphemous words mentioned in verse 5 could be the call for Caesar
worship. Often Christians were forced to curse the name of Christ
and to say Caesar is Lord. Although John does not mention the word
Antichrist in the Book of Revelation, his beast here is often viewed
as such a figure warring against the forces of Christ. This passage
also speaks of the number of people who have been involved in the
Caesar worship, every tribe, people, tongue, and nation. It must have
been very difficult for Christians to resist. We are told, however, that
his rule will be only a short period of time, represented by three and
one-half years (fractions represent incompleteness in the number
code). He will attempt in that short period of time to destroy the
forces of righteousness.

As was indicated earlier, the first four acts of Revelation are cyclical. Many interpreters get so involved in wondering who this beast
will be in AD 1990 or 2000, they miss the beast as it walks across our
earth today. In every age Satan will attempt to use political power
to control the world and to advance his aims. Even as the first
Christians would have viewed this beast as Rome and its government by the Caesars, so in every age Christians have found Satan
lurking in the political process. Christians must always put Romans
13 over against Revelation 13. In Romans 13 the state is praised, and
we are told by Paul to obey the government and to pay our taxes.
Paul wrote those words at a time when the Roman government had
not started active persecution against the Christians. Roman roads
and postal system made Paul's journeys and letters possible. By AD
95 a revolution had taken place, and now Christians were being
actively persecuted by the government. Thus, for John, the Roman
government was the beast.

In every age evil has found some person or some power to advance
its cause. In looking back through world history, one can see powerful governments or dictators who bring great evil to their lands. One

can look back to the Nazi period in Germany and the great evil that was incarnate in Adolf Hitler, and the harm that was brought to the world. We need only to read our newspapers to see the decadence of our human society that is often manifested in the capitals of our nations. History would tell us that the political process is very easily corrupted to become a vehicle to evil rather than good. This type of corrupt political beast will continue to stalk the world as long as the world lasts. What the first Christians experienced in Rome we all experience in every age.

The word *Antichrist* appears only in the Johannine letters of the New Testament, as in 1 John 2:18, "Children, it is the last hour; and as you have heard that antichrist is coming, so now many antichrists have come; therefore, we know that it is the last hour." Any time the word is used, it is almost always in the plural which would support our cyclical view of this scene in Revelation. Every age will have its forces which will war against Christ and often these forces will come in the garb of political power.

Scene 3
The Beast from the Land (13:11-18)

Then I saw another beast which rose out of the earth; it had two horns like a lamb and smoke like a dragon. It exercises all the authority of the first beast in its presence, and makes the earth and its inhabitants worship the first beast, whose mortal wound was healed. It works great signs, even making fire come down from heaven to earth in the sight of men; and by the signs which it is allowed to work in the presence of the beast, it deceives those who dwell on earth, bidding them make an image for the beast which was wounded by the sword and yet lived; and it was allowed to give breath to the image of the beast, so that the image of the beast should even speak, and to cause those who will not worship the image of the beast to be slain. Also it causes all, both small and great, both rich and poor, both free and slave, to be marked on the right hand or on the forehead, so that no one can buy or sell unless he has the mark, that is, the name of the beast or the number of its name. This calls for wisdom; let him who has understanding reckon the number of the beast, for it is as a human number, its number is six hundred and sixty-six.

We have said that the best way for Satan to control the world is to use political power. A second way is to turn political power into a religious service. The beast from the land symbolizes the worship

of political power. This beast comes in the guise of a lamb, except it
has two horns instead of seven and speaks with the authority of the
dragon. In all the cities of Asia Minor there was a council of ten
called the Concilia who was given the authority by Rome to carry out
the Caesar worship. The two horns in contrast to the seven horns of
the lamb stresses the limited power of this beast compared to the
perfect power of the lamb. John states very clearly in verse 12, "It
exercises all the authority of the first beast in its presence, makes
the earth and its inhabitants worship the first beast, whose mortal
wound was healed." Here, we can see very clearly the Caesar worship of Asia Minor. The Concilia required people to worship the
statue, sometimes three times a day, and say "Caesar is Lord." Sometimes Christians were forced to curse the name of Christ.

The largest statue that has been excavated of Caesar Domitian has
been found in the city of Ephesus and is over sixteen feet tall. This
was hollow on the inside so that the priests could go inside and make
the statue talk. We find this hinted at in verse 15, "and it was
allowed to give breath to the image of the beast so that the image
of the beast should even speak, and cause those who will not worship
the image of the beast to be slain." If you worshiped the beast, then
you were tattooed on the back of the hand or on the forehead (see
v. 16). You could not buy or sell in the marketplace unless you had
this sign of the Roman government.

The so-called Mark of the Beast, then, in John's day was this mark
of Caesar worship which allowed one to carry on commerce. In verse
18 we are given the number of the beast as 666. If you translate
Caesar Nero's name into Hebrew, you get the pattern NRON KSR.
In the Hebrew alphabet all the letters were used as numbers, N=50,
R=200, O=6, N=50, K=100, S=60, R=200, or 666. It is quite likely
that John had in mind Caesar Domitian as 666, the incarnation of
Caesar Nero, the beast who had been wounded but who had been
made well.

Again, in a cyclical fashion, in every age we encounter the same
basic truth. Satan will use political power and turn it into a worship
service to control our age. John and the first Christians viewed this
as Rome and the Concilia; however, we have seen it happening over
and over again throughout the ages. Dictators rise and fall and so

often their reigns are imbued with divinity or the trappings of religion.

Recently an old propaganda film of Nazi Germany was shown in a leading city of the United States for a charity function. Citizens of that city went to the museum in their best clothing; they watched the old film which depicted Hitler arrive in Munich, Germany, in an airplane. The shots emphasized the sequence of the airplane going through the white clouds until finally the airplane was out of sight. It is obvious the propagandist wanted to give an aura of messiahship to Hitler. Finally the plane landed and Hitler got off. The newspaper reported that when Hitler got off the plane in the film this charity group in our own country had gotten so caught up in the film that they stood up and cheered for Hitler.

Look at the old Nazi war films and you will see a religious fervor in the eyes of the people as they proclaimed, "Heil, Hitler." The Baptists in Germany learned a very difficult lesson; Hitler used Romans 13 against the Baptist church, telling them that they had to obey the state. In fact, he granted the Baptists certain freedoms they never had before, and some Baptist leaders became firm supporters of Hitler. Perhaps German Baptists were so concerned about who the beast and 666 would be in the future that they overlooked the raging beast of Nazism in their own time.

Throughout the ages people have tried to identify 666. Martin Luther said it was the Pope; the Pope said it was Martin Luther. In the days of the Depression the Republicans said it was Roosevelt; later the Democrats said it was Nixon. On college campuses popular candidates have been Henry Kissinger, Jimmy Carter, and, most recently, Ronald Wilson Reagan, because he has six letters in each of his names. Individuals forget the impact of history itself and overlook what history has to say on the subject. The same is true with the Mark of the Beast. The first Social Security cards were thought by some to be the Mark of the Beast. The plastic credit cards have been indicted as the Mark of the Beast. It is obvious from our study that in the original context the worship of Caesar Domitian or Nero, tattooing on the back of hand or forehead, is what John had in mind for the Mark of the Beast and 666.

In a timeless statement we must realize that in every age Satan will not only use political power but will turn it into a worship service. The Communists claim to be atheists but are in reality some of the world's most religious people. The government has become their religion. It is very important that here in our own country we underline the basic Baptist principle of separation of church and state. We must pray that our government will never be used of evil, but if it were to happen, we would hope that the state and church would not be so closely wedded that the church would be destroyed. The primary principle of Christianity is still the words of Jesus to render to Caesar and to render to God. For Christians, duty to God must always come first, even if it stands opposed to what the government has to say. There is a place for Christian patriotism in every country of the world, but there is also a place for the brotherhood of Christians which transcends nations and governments. There is an implied warning in this section of Revelation which would teach us against civil religion, a religion that so associates with the government that one finds it difficult to find a line of separation.

Let us now meet Caesar Domitian, the beast of Revelation.

DOMITIAN: Good day. I am Caesar Domitian. I was born on the 24th of October AD 51 on Pomegranate Street in Rome. My father's name was Vespasian. My childhood was rather poverty stricken, and I led a rather degraded youth. I married Domitia, who had been the wife of Aelius Lamia. As a young man I dreamed of planning an expedition against Gaul in Germany but was dissuaded from doing this by my friends. When my father Vespasian died, my brother Titus was named Caesar. I was very jealous of him and plotted constantly behind his back. Finally, he suddenly fell ill and died. I became Caesar in AD 81. At the beginning of my reign I spent much time reclining on the couches, stabbing flies with a needle-sharp pin. I produced many extravagant entertainments in the coliseum and in the circus for my friends. I even staged a sea battle in the coliseum. At the end of the battle the whole floor of the arena was red with blood. I also had wild beast hunts and gladiator shows. I began a building campaign to restore many important buildings in Rome, errecting a temple to Jupiter, the guardian on the Capitoline Hill, a concert hall, and an artificial lake for sea battles. I also had some success in battle, especially in Germany.

I brought about a number of social innovations, restoring the custom of holding formal dinners, and prohibiting actors from appearing on stage. Through the years I came to the realization that I was divine. This was revealed to me by Zeus. It was important that this word be spread across the Roman Empire. I believed it would be a way of holding together all the far-flung provinces. I sent out orders that statues of myself should be erected and the people should bow down and worship me as divine, saying, "Caesar is Lord." My letters began with the phrase, "Our Lord and God instructs you to do this." Thus, the titles *Lord* and *God* became my regular titles in writing and conversation. In Asia Minor those who worshiped me had to be marked with a tattoo of my face upon their forehead and on the back of the hand; this was the only way they could buy food in the marketplace. Those who refused to worship the statue were severely persecuted. I renamed two months of the year, September and October, the months of my accession to the throne of emperor, and called them Germanicus and Domitian.

During these years I was very fearful of my own life, discovering that my wife and friends were plotting behind my back to put me to death. These fears became reality as I was stabbed in my bedroom on September 18, AD 96; I was 44 years of age and had reigned over Rome for 15 years. My body was taken by my old nurse Phyllis to a garden outside the city on the Latin Way and cremated. My rule over Rome was a very important one, and I left my mark on its history.

Thank you Domitian, for being with us.

Scene 4
The Fourth Tableau—The Lamb with 144,000 (14:1-5)

Then I looked, and lo, on Mount Zion stood the Lamb, and with him a hundred and forty-four thousand who had his name and his Father's name written on their foreheads. And I heard a voice from heaven like the sound of many waters and like the sound of loud thunder; the voice I heard was like the sound of harpers playing on their harps, and they sing a new song before the throne and before the four living creatures and before the elders. No one could learn that song except the hundred and forty-four thousand who had been redeemed from the earth. It is these who have not defiled themselves with women, for they are chaste; it is these who follow the Lamb wherever he goes; these have been redeemed from mankind as first fruits for God and the Lamb, and in their mouth no lie was found, for they are spotless.

The focus of our attention now turns from the forces of evil to the forces of good. The Lamb stands with all true Christians (144,000) on Mount Zion. That mountain was located in Jerusalem, in the upper city, and was considered to be a very holy place because the tomb of David was located there. Often the word *Zion* was used as a term for Jerusalem. The Lamb, of course, is Christ. What greater assurance and hope can Christians have than to know that Christ will be the leader in the battle between good and evil. Satan may have his demonic forces and monster beasts, but the Lamb stands at the head of the Christian army. In contrast to the two-horned lamb in Scene 3, Christ is represented by a Lamb with seven horns and seven eyes, divine power and divine seeing. The 144,000, just as in chapter 7, represent all true Christians, based upon the number 12 × 12, wholeness in the number code. This group bears the mark of Christ in their foreheads, just as the unrighteous under the leadership of Satan carry the Mark of the Beast. These people of the Lamb sing a beautiful hymn of victory. Only those who have been redeemed are able to sing the hymn.

The 144,000 are with the Lamb and sing with him because "they have not defiled themselves with women, they are chaste." John is referring here to the fact that these have not participated in the immoral worship services in the temple of Diana and other such deities. Throughout the Old Testament we often find reference to Israel's marriage to God and any departing from that as adultery. Also we are told "in their mouth no lie was found." In other words, they had not bowed to Domitan's statue and confessed "Caesar is Lord." John may also have had in mind here the regulations for soldiers going into war found in Deuteronomy (23:9ff). There soldiers are called upon to be pure in every way, especially in reference to ceremonial cleanliness. This may be why John has viewed these soldiers with Christ as male virgins. However, we are to see the group as symbolizing the whole church, male and female. The firstfruits mentioned in verse 4 signifies the harvest being offered unto God. Here, the 144,000 are the firstfruits of all mankind offered up to God and the Lamb.

Interlude: Announcement of the Three Angels (14:6-13)

Then I saw another angel flying in midheaven, with an eternal gospel to proclaim to those who dwell on earth, to every nation and tribe and tongue and people; and he said with a loud voice, "Fear God and give him glory, for the hour of his judgment has come; and worship him who made heaven and earth, the sea and the fountains of water."

Another angel, a second, followed, saying, "Fallen, fallen is Babylon the great, she who made all nations drink the wine of her impure passion."

And another angel, a third, followed saying with a loud voice, "If any one worships the beast and its image, and receives a mark on his forehead or on his hand, he also shall drink the wine of God's wrath, poured unmixed into the cup of his anger, and he shall be tormented with fire and brimstone in the presence of the holy angels and in the presence of the Lamb. And the smoke of their torment goes up for ever and ever; and they have no rest, day or night, these worshipers of the beast and its image, and whoever receives the mark of its name."

Here is a call for the endurance of the saints, those who keep the commandments of God and the faith of Jesus. And I heard a voice from heaven saying, "Write this: Blessed are the dead who die in the Lord henceforth." "Blessed indeed," says the Spirit, "that they may rest from their labors, for their deeds follow them!"

An angel flies through heaven to announce an eternal gospel to those who are living on earth. This angel's message is a call to people on earth to worship God and give him glory. It is now time for his judgment to come upon the world. The victory of the Lamb is so definite that even before the battle begins this angel can declare the news of victory. In the ancient world when the Greeks won a battle there was no way to get news back to Athens except to send a runner. Sometime he would run all night long, then burst through the city gates crying, "We have won the victory." This angel flies across the heavens in a similar fashion, declaring the great victory even before it happens.

The second angel announces the fall of Babylon the great. Throughout biblical literature Babylon symbolizes a wicked power. In the Old Testament Babylon was the ancient enemy of the Jewish people. Babylon leveled Solomon's Temple to the ground and led the Jews into captivity. In Revelation, Babylon is a code name for Rome, a power as evil as ancient Babylon itself. (See Isa. 21:9; Dan. 4:27.) John views the evil influence of Rome as sharing her wine of impure passion to all the people of the world.

In 14:9-11 there is a message of doom to the people living on earth. The wrath of God will come upon any who fall down to worship the statue of the beast and receive its mark. In John's day Christians were tempted to worship Caesar's statue and confess him as Lord in order to buy food for their families. Some were even teaching that it was possible to worship both Caesar and Jesus Christ. The gnostic group especially taught that the body and soul were separate. In Revelation these people are called Nicolaitans. Thus one could bow down to Caesar in the body and the soul and not be affected and still be able to confess Jesus Christ as Lord.

A strong warning is imparted here by John. Anyone who worships the beast must also participate in its punishment. "He shall be tormented with fire and brimstone in the presence of the holy angels and in the presence of the Lamb." Verse 11 tells us that this torment will be eternal. What a contrast this provides! Refusing to bow down to Caesar's statue might bring momentary persecution or even at worst a martyr's death, but such is no comparison to the eternal punishment of God on those who receive the mark of Caesar upon their bodies.

Christians in John's time needed such a warning to avoid giving in to the enemy. Someone who gave in to Caesar worship just to fill his stomach would encounter eternal punishment. Thus John gives the admonition to the righteous, "don't give in to Caesar worship," or as expressed in verse 12, "Here is a call for the endurance of the saints, those who keep the commandments of God and the faith of Jesus." John did not want to see the Christians surrender in the last hour. Those Christians who were willing to die as martyrs, to fight on to the end, would be especially blessed. "Write this, Blessed are the dead who die in the Lord henceforth" (v. 13). Throughout Revelation, but especially in the latter part of chapter 7, we see the blessing of the martyrs as they march into heaven to receive their heavenly rewards.

Scene 5
The Fifth Tableau—The Son of Man on a Cloud (14:14-16)

Then I looked, and lo, a white cloud, and seated on the cloud one like a son of man, with a golden crown on his head, and a sharp sickle in his hand. And another angel came out of the temple, calling with a loud voice to him who sat upon the cloud, "Put in your sickle and reap, for the hour to reap has come, for the harvest of the earth is fully ripe." So he who sat upon the cloud swung his sickle on the earth, and the earth was reaped.

Satan has two monster beasts to carry out his evil work upon the face of the earth. In Scenes 5 and 6 we encounter the forces on the side of the righteous. The first of these is expressed here in scene five, the judgment of the Son of Man. The sickle stands as a symbol of divine judgment. The symbolism of judgment is based strictly upon Joel 3:13. However, Christ is described as the Son of Man, depending very heavily upon Daniel 7:13. A crown on his head establishes that he is Lord, the Messiah, and King. An angel comes directly from the Temple of God and declares that judgment should begin. Reaping and harvesting are terms throughout the Bible to stand for judgment. Here the gathering in of the grain might indicate separation of the righteous from the unrighteous.

Scene 6
The Sixth Tableau—The Harvest of Grapes (14:17-20)

And another angel came out of the temple in heaven, and he too had a sharp sickle. Then another angel came out from the altar, the angel who has power over fire, he called with a loud voice to him who had the sharp sickle, "Put in your sickle, and gather the clusters of the vine of the earth, for its grapes are ripe." So the angel swung his sickle on the earth and gathered the vintage of the earth, and threw it into the great wine press of the wrath of God; and the wine press was trodden outside the city and blood flowed from the winepress, as high as a horse's bridle, for one thousand six hundred stadia.

Both Scenes 5 and 6 stress judgment as God's handiwork and as a tool for the righteous. The harvesting of the wheat and the grapes doubles the image. In many parts of Europe today grapes are still gathered in a great vat, and women and children trample out the grapes with their bare feet, much as they did in ancient Palestine. This image is used here, but instead of juice coming out of the vat, blood comes forth up to a horse's bridle and sixteen hundred stadia long. The impact of the picture is to show that the great judgment of God, when it does come, will be universal. Blood might also represent the blood of the martyrs who must die in the last days.

Sixteen hundred stadia may symbolize the length of ancient Palestine. From Tyre to El-Arisch near Egypt is 1,664 stadia. Jewish writers were inclined to describe warfare in such exaggerated terms (see 1 Enoch 100:1ff and 2 Esdras 15:35ff). God will bring his judgment upon the earth, and no one will be able to resist him. His judgment will be total and complete.

Scene 7
The Seventh Tableau—The Hymn of the Lamb (15:1-4)

Then I saw another portent in heaven, great and wonderful, seven angels with seven plagues, which are the last, for with them the wrath of God is ended. And I saw what appeared to be a sea of glass mingled with fire, and those who had conquered the beast and its image and the number of its name, standing by the sea of glass with harps of God in their hands. And they sing the song of Moses, the servant of God, and the song of the Lamb, saying,
"Great and wonderful are thy deeds,
O Lord God the Almighty!
Just and true are thy ways,
O king of the ages!
Who shall not fear and glorify thy name, O Lord?
For thou alone art holy,
All nations shall come and worship thee,
for thy judgments have been revealed."

In this act showing the struggle between good and evil, we see the martyrs gathered around the throne of God beside the sea of glass singing a beautiful hymn of victory. The 7 angels bearing 7 plagues also come out on stage and prepare for the opening of Act V. Throughout Act IV we have seen the struggle between Satan and his 2 monster beasts opposing Christ and the true believers. At the end of Act IV we are convinced that the victory of Christ is secure; even though the battle has not come, we can sing of victory for the side of the righteous. Who can persevere against the Lamb and his sickle of judgment?

The sea of glass is mingled with fire to symbolize the judgment that is now ready to come upon the face of the earth. The song which they sing is called the song of Moses. It is a beautiful hymn of praise to God, the righteous King, who brings deliverance. Those in the 7 churches who read this passage would find inner strength to persevere through the difficult days that were about to come upon the earth, to behold their fallen brethren in heaven and see them rejoicing in hymn and in music. The sea of glass has become something of a heavenly Red Sea. The martyrs now rejoice in song.

Two hymns are ascribed to Moses in the Old Testament, one as the children of Israel stood by the Red Sea praising God for his deliverance (Ex. 15:1-22), the other near the end of the life of Moses (Deuteronomy 32). It is obvious that John has in mind here the deliverance at the Red Sea; yet both hymns need to be considered in the Revelation hymn (vv. 1-2 and 3-4). All the nations will stand in fear at the name of God, bowing down before his throne. This would have brought a message of great hope to the Christians who were being persecuted by Rome; the image of Rome coming to bow down before the throne of Christ would have uplifted their spirits. Now they were being forced to bow down to the throne of Rome; soon the tables would turn.

In this act we have seen the struggle between good and evil all through world history. The forces of evil will be led by Satan and his helpers, depicted as monster beasts representing political power and the worship of political power. Against the forces of evil, Christ leads the 144,000, all true Christians. At their side will be Christ as the judge with the judgment of God brought upon the face of the earth. The act ends on a note of music, singing of God's glory in heaven as the martyrs have already won the victory even though the battle has not taken place. The curtain leading into the holy of holies was parted to show us the ark of the covenant, symbolizing God's promises down through the ages. Now at the end of the act the curtain begins to draw closed as we are preparing for the 7 final judgments of God upon the earth.

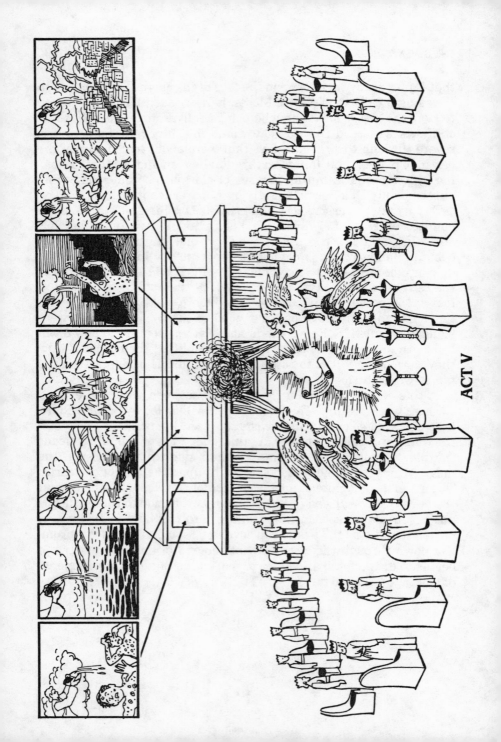

ACT V

Act V
The Seven Bowls of Wrath

Revelation 15:5 to 16:21

Stage Setting

The orchestra level remains the same as in the previous 4 acts. God's throne is set at center stage, surrounded by the 4 living creatures and the 24 elders. Seven burning lampstands still burn before the throne, and the sea of glass separates the orchestra level from the audience. At the bottom of the stage building one sees a door leading into the holy of holies of the Jewish Temple. Seven angels come out of the door, and as soon as they leave the Temple we can no longer see the ark of the covenant, for the holy of holies is filled with smoke. The 7 angels, robed in pure white linen, girded about with golden girdles, proceed to the ledge of the stage (*proskene*) and station themselves before the 7 windows. Each angel, then, in turn walks to the edge of the ledge of the stage and pours out his bowl upon the lower stage. Immediately behind him in the window we see a scene of full judgment upon the earth. The other angels continue with the full plagues of God. This is the fastest moving act in Revelation. Once God's final judgment comes upon the earth, it will be quick and to the point.

The Jewish Temple

In each act of Revelation there is a scene from the Jewish Temple. So far we have encountered the seven-branch candlestick, the altar of incense, the altar of sacrifice, and the ark of the covenant. In Act V we encounter the closing of the holy of holies and its being filled with smoke. The 7 angels leave the holy of holies and the smoke prohibits us from looking into it again. The sea of glass turns red with fire. Everything about the stage setting and the scene from the Temple suggests the coming wrath and judgment of God upon the earth. Then a loud voice from the Temple shouts to the 7 angels, "Go and pour out on the earth the seven bowls of the wrath of God" (16:1).

Spiral Action

At the beginning of our study, we indicated that John wedded together two views of history, the cyclical from Greek tragic drama, and the straight line from Hebraic prophetic literature, producing a spiral effect. The first 4 acts of Revelation have been cyclical like wheels spinning around, the scenes going by as a carousel going around. Yet at the same time as the wheel of history is turning in Revelation, it is also moving forward, producing a spiral effect. You may have had the experience of circling an airport waiting to land. Even as the plane circled, it moved forward. Act V brings us to this forward movement, pointing toward the end of history or a goal for mankind as the complete judgment of God is poured out upon the world. In contrast to Act III, everything is complete. Act III emphasized one third of things being destroyed, whereas Act V brings the fulfillment of these. Acts III and V should be placed next to one another, as well as Acts IV and VI, for they are interrelated. Each of the 7 scenes in Act III is intensified in Act V. For example, in Act III the first plague did not come upon mankind until Scene 5, the plague of the locusts. In Act V the very first scene brings a plague of ulcerous sores upon mankind. In Trumpet 1 the greenery of the earth was damaged by a plague of hail and rain mixed with fire. In Bowl 1 we have human beings being afflicted with ulcerous sores. In Trumpet 2 one third of the sea became blood; in Bowl 2 all the sea becomes the blood of a dead man. In Trumpet 3 one third of the fresh water became bitter; in Bowl 3 all of the fresh water becomes bitter. In Trumpet 4 one third of the heavenly bodies lost their light; in Bowl 4 the sun intensifies its light and burns the inhabitants on earth. In Trumpet 5 a plague of locusts tormented one third of the earth; in Bowl 5 there is a plague of darkness which brings pain—a fact which implies the locusts are still at work. Trumpet 6 brought about a plague of barbarians at the Euphrates River; in Bowl 6 the kings of the earth march down the dry riverbed of the Euphrates river to bring about the last battle on earth. Trumpet 7 introduced a hymn of rejoicing for God's judgment, and Bowl 7 brought about the total destruction of the earth by a great earthquake and large hail. Act III in many ways was a warning of things to come, and Act V fulfills this in every detail.

John symbolizes in Act V the quickly executed wrath of God on the Roman Empire. It took courage and steadfast faith for John to write these words, because as they were being written Rome was still very strong and in no danger of falling. He believed that with the end of the Roman Empire, the end of the world would take place and the return of Jesus Christ. He had received the revelation of God and was now sharing it with his people. In a timeless, cyclical sense we hear the truth that political power used of evil will be overturned, and the age will come to an end. As we saw in Act III, all the forces of nature rebelled against the sin of mankind bringing the full destruction of the earth.

Scene 1
The First Bowl—Curse on the Earth (16:2)

So the first angel went and poured his bowl upon the earth, and foul and evil sores came upon the men who bore the mark of the beast and worshiped its image.

This bowl is much more intense than the first trumpet in that the plague comes immediately upon mankind. This plague of ulcers is very similar to the sixth Egyptian plague of boils. In Exodus 9:8-12, we find Moses and Aaron throwing ashes into the air to cover the land of Egypt which brought about terrible boils and sores upon the men and beasts. The first bowl plague comes only upon those who have been marked by the beast, those who have fallen down and worshiped its image. Again we see the importance of the sealing of the Christians. These plagues will not come upon them. It is a fitting plague for those who have worshiped the beast and received its image upon their forehead or upon the back of their hands, for the ulcers are manifested in their physical bodies. They are punished in the very realm where they sinned.

Scene 2
The Second Bowl—Curse on the Sea (16:3)

The second angel poured his bowl into the sea, and it became like the blood of a dead man, and every living thing died that was in the sea.

John, standing on Patmos, looked out and beheld the beautiful
Aegean Sea; it seemed only fitting that the next plague should come
upon the sea. All of the sea became blood, not just regular blood, but
the blood of a dead person or murdered person. Every living being
in contact with the sea died. This plague is similar to the first Egyptian plague in which the water of the Nile was turned to blood,
causing the water to be foul and killing all of the fish (Ex. 7:14-25).
The judgment of God has become more intensified. Each time the
cycle turns, an intensification takes place in the Book of Revelation.
It is like looking at a carousel and watching the horses turn around
and around. At some moment in time it will turn for the last time;
for John that will be the most intense turning of the wheel leading
to the last days.

Scene 3
The Third Bowl—Curse on the Rivers (16:4-7)

The third angel poured his bowl into the rivers and fountains of water,
and they became blood. And I heard the angel of water say,
    "Just art thou in these thy judgments,
    thou who art and wast, O Holy One.
    For men have shed the blood of saints and prophets,
    and thou has given them blood to drink.
    It is their due!"
And I heard the altar cry,
    "Yea, Lord God the Almighty,
    true and just are thy judgments!"

Instead of the water becoming bitter (one third of it in the trumpet
vision), now all of the fresh water becomes polluted and turns to
blood. The Jewish people had a strict food law concerning eating
meat with blood in it. All the blood had to be drained out before it
was considered kosher. It would have been very repugnant for anyone from a Jewish background to consider all of the fresh water and
springs becoming blood. Very strangely, even the angel who was in
charge of the springs of water agreed with this judgment brought
upon the earth. Throughout Revelation there are angels in charge
of such things as the altar and natural elements. The Jews believed
that angels were ministering spirits and were given certain kinds of

duties to perform. They play an important and strategic role all the way through the Book of Revelation. The angel in charge of the springs of water utters the view that it is only fitting that the people who have spilled the blood of the martyrs should have blood to drink. Lynn Hough said, "Men cannot attack the friends of God and expect God's world to be their friend. Its very fountains will become fountains of death." We find a similar feeling in Wisdom 11:5ff that it was fitting that the Nile plague come upon the Egyptians for the murders of the Hebrew children.

Scene 4
The Fourth Bowl—Curse on the Sun (16:8-9)

> The fourth angel poured his bowl on the sun, and it was allowed to scorch men with fire; men were scorched by the fierce heat, and they cursed the name of God who has power over these plagues, and they did not repent and give him glory.

Instead of the heavenly bodies losing their light as in the trumpet visions, the sun intensifies its heat. In 2 Peter 3:10 we find the words: "But the day of the Lord will come like a thief, and then the heavens will pass away with a loud noise, and the elements will be dissolved with fire, and the earth and the works that are upon it will be burned up." The sun which was once a friend to man has now become an enemy. Those who have made God their enemy find no friend in the universe or its elements.

In contrast, the true Christians are not affected by this plague. They have been given the promise, "the sun shall not strike them, nor any scorching heat" (Rev. 7:16). The Israelites were protected during the Egyptian plague. When the Egyptians had no light, the Israelites had light (Ex. 10:23). Also, just like the aftermath of the Egyptian plague there is no repentance here after the first four bowls of wrath. The people curse the name of God rather than uttering words of repentance; they recognize God's power over the plague but did not give him glory. As Beasley-Murray said, "The mark of the beast on their bodies has penetrated their souls, instilling in them the hostility towards God and his holiness which is characteristic of the beast himself."

Scene 5
The Fifth Bowl—Curse on the Beast's Throne (16:10-11)

The fifth angel poured his bowl on the throne of the beast and its kingdom was in darkness; men gnawed their tongues in anguish and cursed the God of heaven for their pain and sores, and did not repent of their deeds.

This bowl reminds us of the eighth Egyptian plague of darkness upon the land. However, we encounter something more than darkness here. It is darkness which brings pain with it. John has in mind the same darkness which shrouded the sun when the locusts came up out of the abyss in Act III (9:2). That darkness is still present here, but is intensified by the presence of the demonic locusts bringing great pain on the kingdom of the beast. Although darkness is the only thing mentioned in Bowl 5, one should presume all of the other influences from Trumpet 5. This is one of the most awesome scenes in all of the Book of Revelation. There is nothing left but pain and suffering. The kingdom of the beast—Rome itself—is the subject of this paralyzing darkness; more than any other kingdom it had brought terror and hardship to the Christians. However, even all of the pain of the bowl plagues does not bring Rome to repentance. Wisdom of Solomon 17:3-5 expresses it well.

Thinking that their secret sins might escape detection beneath a dark pall of oblivion, they lay in disorder, dreadfully afraid, terrified by apparitions. For the dark corner that held them offered no refuge from fear, but loud, unnerving noises roared around them, and phantoms with downcast unsmiling faces passed before their eyes. No fire, however great, had force enough to give them light, nor had the brilliant flaming stars strength to illuminate that hideous darkness.

Scene 6
The Sixth Bowl—Curse on the Euphrates (16:12-16)

The sixth angel poured his bowl on the great river Euphrates, and its water was dried up, to prepare the way for the kings from the east. And I saw issuing from the mouth of the dragon and from the mouth of the beast and from the mouth of the false prophets, three foul spirits like frogs; for they are demonic spirits, performing signs, who go abroad to the kings of the whole world, to assemble them for battle on the great day of God the Almighty. (Lo, "I am coming like a thief! Blessed is he who is awake, keeping his garments that he may not go naked and be seen exposed!") And they assembled them at the place which was called in Hebrew Armageddon.

In Trumpet 6, the Euphrates River was featured on center stage; in Bowl 6, three frogs go forth from the mouths of Satan and his helper monster beasts at the Euphrates to summon the kings together for the last struggle between good and evil. In the animal code the frog represents the most vile and evil of all creatures. In the Zen religion, frogs were considered to be the cause of all plagues and death. In the Babylonian religions frogs were viewed as the agent of Ahriman, an evil figure. In our passage we find that they also bring evil upon the world. The ancient people feared the frog and were apprehensive whenever they saw one.

Herodotus, the great Greek historian, tells us that on one occasion the Euphrates River actually did dry up during the time of Cyrus the Persian. Cyrus had tried for nearly a year to conquer Babylon, which was built over the Euphrates River and consequently had a constant water supply. Finally, in frustration, Cyrus took a group of his soldiers and went into the interior and diverted the flow of the Euphrates River, thus drying up the riverbed. Then he used the dry riverbed as an open avenue into the heart of Babylon and took the city. The same Cyrus allowed the Jews to return home after his capture of the city.

Isaiah also prophesied:

> And the Lord will utterly destroy
>   the tongue of the sea of Egypt;
> and will wave his hand over the River
>   with his scorching wind,
> and smite it into seven channels
>   that man may cross dryshod (11:15).

In Zechariah, we find the words: "They shall pass through the sea of Egypt, and the waves of the sea shall be smitten, and all the depths of the Nile dried up" (10:11). In these Old Testament references, the motif of the drying up of the water is viewed as God intervening to save his people Israel. Here in Revelation, the dry riverbed will become the avenue for destruction and terror. The invading kings will be as horrible as the ancient Parthians, the dreaded enemy of Rome. One must also remember that the Roman army which destroyed Jerusalem in AD 70 contained three thousand Parthian recruits.

These forces gather together at a place called Armageddon. Revelation 16:16 is the only place where the actual battlefield is mentioned. The battlefield likely received its name from the city of Megiddo (Har Mageddon—Hill of Megiddo) which guarded a large plain in Northern Israel, triangular in shape, 15×15×20 miles. We have invited the mayor of Megiddo, to tell us something about his ancient city.

MAYOR SIMEON: Our city is located on a spur of the Carmel range which juts onto the plain of Esdraelon. Our city was built on this strategic location to guard the main highway leading from Egypt along the coast of Palestine. At present-day Haifa, it cut westward by Megiddo across the plain of Esdraelon toward Babylon. From the heights of our city one could see the whole plain northward to Galilee and westward to Mt. Gilboa. Our city was founded in the early fourth millennium BC and over twenty civilizations have lived at this site.

We are most proud of our famous water tunnel. It is over 2,800 years old and pierces into the earth 127 feet. It was built to connect with a tunnel 215 feet long which leads to a hidden spring outside the city's wall. In time of warfare the women can safely journey to the spring to bring water to our citizens. Many major events in Jewish history have taken place on the plain of Esdraelon stretching before our city. In the time of the Judges, Deborah defeated Sisera at the Kishon River (Judg. 6:19-20). King Saul lost a major battle there and took his life on Mt. Gilboa. Solomon fortified the city as a chariot city and had over 450 horses and 150 chariots stationed there (1 Kings 9:15), Ahaziah, king of Israel was slain here by Jehu (2 Kings 9:27), and Joshua was killed by Pharaoh Neco (2 Kings 23:29-30). Battles were fought here during the Maccabean period, during Napoleon's time, during the British era under General Allenby and during the Six Day War of 1967. General Eisenhower once stood there and pronounced it a classic battlefield.

Thank you Mayor Simeon of Megiddo.
It is no wonder that John then takes the name Armageddon as a

symbolic name for the last struggle between good and evil. It stands as a demonic counterpart to the mount of God. The war that John was expecting would not be in northern Israel but rather Rome. John warns his readers in verse 15, that the last days of Rome would come suddenly. Christians should be prepared for those days. The coming of Christ would also be like a thief in the night.

Scene 7
The Seventh Bowl—Curse on the Air (16:17-21)

The seventh angel poured his bowl into the air, and a great voice came out of the temple, from the throne, saying, "It is done!" And there were flashes of lightning, voices, peals of thunder, and a great earthquake such as had never been since men were on the earth, so great was that earthquake. The great city was split into three parts, and the cities of the nations fell, and God remembered great Babylon, to make her drain the cup of the fury of his wrath. And every island fled away, and no mountains were to be found; and great hailstones, heavy as a hundredweight, dropped on men from heaven, till men cursed God for the plague of hail, so fearful was that plague.

Cosmic upheaval characterizes the end of the age. This will herald the arrival of Christ and the establishment of his kingdom. Haggai declares: "Once again, in a little while, I will shake the heavens and the earth and the sea and the dry land" (Hag. 2:6). Rome had persecuted the saints and martyrs of God. It would get exactly what it deserved. Again John is using Babylon as a code name for Rome. God uses a mighty earthquake to bring about her destruction. John viewed the fall of Babylon as bringing the end of the age. He will give us a detailed version of that fall in chapters 17—18. In the Old Testament, earthquakes were often associated with the judgment of God. "And you shall flee as you fled from the earthquake in the day of Uzziah king of Judah. Then the Lord your God will come, and all the holy ones with him" (Zech. 14:5). The destruction of islands and mountains also become symbols of the final judgment. Rome, of course, was known for its famous seven mountains.

A large hailstone shatters the city of Rome signaling the end. Yet the wicked of the city remain to curse the name of God. It will still be some time until the Lord returns ending human history. Throughout the centuries various prophets have seen their own historical crisis as a prelude to the end. From the very first of Revelation, Rome has been doomed for the ill treatment of Christians. In a timeless cyclical sense, we are being taught that any nation opposing God will encounter his judgment. Each age is to live in the expectancy of the return of Christ.

Act V as we have seen is fast paced—not one interlude intervenes. When God decides to judge Babylon, his judgment is swift. In contrast to Act III, the judgment is total and more intensified. The very first bowl of wrath effects mankind—ulcerous sores. The spiral time effect of Revelation moves rapidly toward the end times. The act ends with Babylon and Rome in ruins. Act VI will bring us the full impact of that destruction.

Act VI
The Seven Judgments

Revelation 17:1 to 20:3

Stage Setting

The stage setting for this act takes place in the seven great windows (*thuromata*) of the Ephesian stage. The seven judgments of God will be demonstrated in these windows. The orchestra level remains the same as in the previous acts. God's throne is set in center stage surrounded by the four living creatures and the twenty-four elders. Seven lampstands still burn before the throne, and a sea of glass separates the orchestra level from the audience. In back of the throne room scene looms the Jewish Temple with the curtains closed leading to the holy of holies. It is shrouded in the smoke going up from the city's rubble, burning in the foreground. The choir sings several funeral dirges and laments over the burning city. The first 3 scenes of this act set forth a long, detailed description of the fall of Rome. More emphasis is placed upon this theme than any other one in the Book of Revelation. John devotes 3 verses to the Battle of Armageddon, 4 verses to the Millennium, and nearly 2 whole chapters (17—18) to the fall of Rome.

The Jewish Temple

Each act of Revelation has a theme from the Jewish Temple; so far we have encountered the seven-branch candlestick, the altar of incense, the altar of sacrifice, and the ark of the covenant. In Act 6 the whole stage building becomes the Jewish Temple. In many of the great tragic dramas the stage building could serve as a house, temple, or some other public building. The major emphasis, however, is upon the burning city of Rome. The Temple appears in the smoke behind the throne of God.

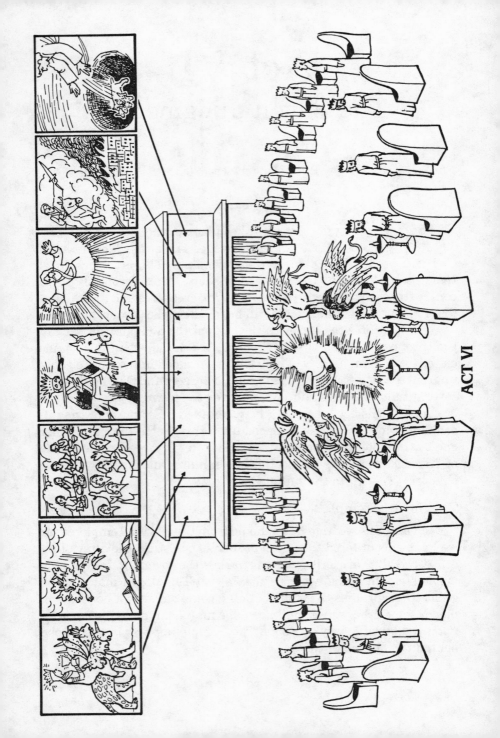

ACT VI

Scene 1
The First Judgment—The Woman and the Scarlet Beast
(17:1-18)

Then one of the seven angels who had the seven bowls came and said to me, "Come, I will show you the judgment of the great harlot who is seated upon many waters, with whom the kings of the earth have committed fornication, and with the wine of whose fornication the dwellers on earth have become drunk." And he carried me away in the Spirit, into a wilderness, and I saw a woman sitting on a scarlet beast which was full of blasphemous names, and it had seven heads and ten horns. The woman was arrayed in purple and scarlet and bedecked with gold and jewels and pearls, holding in her hand a golden cup full of abominations and the impurities of her fornication; and on her forehead was written a name of mystery: "Babylon the great, mother of harlots and of earth's abominations." And I saw the woman, drunk with the blood of the saints and the blood of the martyrs of Jesus.

When I saw her I marveled greatly. But the angel said to me, "Why marvel? I will tell you the mystery of the woman, and of the beast with seven heads and ten horns that carries her. The beast that you saw was, and is not, and is to ascend from the bottomless pit and go to perdition; and the dwellers on earth whose names have not been written in the book of life from the foundation of the world, will marvel to behold the beast, because it was and is not and is to come. This calls for a mind with wisdom: the seven heads are seven mountains on which the woman is seated; they are also seven kings, five of whom have fallen, one is, the other has not yet come, and when he comes he must remain only a little while. As for the beast that was and is not, it is an eighth but it belongs to the seventh, and it goes to perdition. And the ten horns that you saw are ten kings who have not yet received royal power, but they are to receive authority as kings for one hour, together with the beast. These are of one mind and give over their power and authority to the beast; they will make war on the Lamb, and the Lamb will conquer them, for he is Lord of lords and King of kings, and those with him are called chosen and faithful."

And he said to me, "Thee waters that you saw, where the harlot is seated, are peoples and multitudes and nations and tongues. And the ten horns that you saw, they and the beast will hate the harlot; they will make her desolate and naked, and devour her flesh and burn her up with fire, for God has put it into their hearts to carry out his purpose by being of one mind and give over their royal power to the beast, until the words of God shall be fulfilled. And the woman that you saw is the great city which has dominion over the kings of the earth."

John begins the act with a very fitting symbol for Rome. She is portrayed as a great harlot, dressed in the gaudy garments which were typical of the first-century world, purple and scarlet in color. Purple cloth was very expensive and hard to find. Scarlet in the color code is a symbol for immorality. The harlot is bedecked with gold jewels and pearls. She holds in her hand a golden cup which is filled not with wine but with the abomination and impurities of her trade. She is stamped on the head with the phrase, "Babylon the great, mother of harlots and of earth's abominations." Many of the harlots in Rome were branded on the forehead with the word *porne* which meant prostitute. Often, their heads would be shaved as well. "A golden cup full of abominations" might well refer to the obscenities used in Caesar worship, typical of AD 95. The harlot's cup is also filled with the blood of the martyrs who have already been killed in the persecutions.

"Seated upon many waters" would symbolize Rome as the great seaport town of the world. In addition, the kings of the earth have journeyed to commit fornication with her and to participate in the wine poured from her cup. Rome was the world's capital; her influence extended to every part of the world around the Mediterranean Sea. The woman is seated on a scarlet beast; the beast symbolizes the Roman Empire and the woman represents Rome, the great capital of the empire. The beast had seven heads and ten horns. There had been seven Caesars from the time of the death of Jesus to the time of Domitian. They were Tiberius, AD 14-37; Caligula, AD 37-41; Claudius, AD 41-54; Nero, AD 54-68; Vespasian, AD 69-79; Titus, AD 79-81; and Domitian, AD 81-96. The ten horns stand for the complete power of the Roman Empire.

In many ways Acts IV and VI are in parallel forms. Act IV began with the portrayal of the woman standing on the moon, representing mother Israel. Act VI commences with the portrayal of a woman, the great harlot riding on the monster beast of Rome. The woman standing on the moon brings forth a child who, in turn, brings salvation to the world. The harlot on the beast, in turn, brings death and destruction to the earth. The woman standing on the moon flees to the desert for safekeeping and security. The harlot resides in the desert, consorts with the devil and evil spirits.

In verses 7-14 John breaks the apocalyptic code and tells who these animals symbolize. In part he does this by presenting a riddle which would have been difficult for the Romans to interpret, but would have been obvious to the Christians in the 7 churches. The beast carrying the woman is Rome, more precisely Domitian as a reincarnation of Nero, the most evil of the Roman kings. The empire is now ready to suffer destruction. There had been seven kings, Tiberius, Caligula, Claudius, Nero, Vespasian, Titus, Domitian. Three are left out, Galba, Otho, and Vitellius because all three served within a one-year period of time after Nero. Five have fallen, Tiberius, Caligula, Claudius, Vespasian, and Titus. "The who is" is Domitian; "the one who is yet to come" is Nero, who will return as an evil person to rule over the earth. In actuality he will reincarnate himself in the form of the reigning emperor, Domitian, and continue only a little while, then go onto destruction. He is an eighth king but also one of the seven. He is, in actuality, the beast incarnate, coming up from the pit to bring evil upon the world.

The 10 horns of the beast might well be the 10 Parthian kings or, perhaps in a more general sense, the 10 horns symbolize the line of kings who will precede the Antichrist (see Daniel 7:7). However, in contrast to Daniel, the 10 kings of Revelation are at work with the Antichrist in an unholy alliance between the Neronian forces and the kings of the world to persecute the church and the Christians. Nero, returning from the East, perhaps with the Eastern kings and the Parthians, will make war on the harlot, the city of Rome. Civil warfare breaks out within the land. The whole city is stripped of its wealth and then devoured by fire.

John sees God at work in using these Eastern kings to destroy Rome because of the evil which has been in the city. The forces of Satan end up carrying out the will of God. The ruins of Rome stand as tombstones reminding us of her evil and the great judgment of God upon her. Rome would one day emerge again on the scene, this time as the headquarters of the Christian church.

Scene 2
The Second Judgment—The Fall of Babylon (18:1-24)

After this I saw another angel coming down from heaven, having great authority; and the earth was made bright with his splendor. And he called out with a mighty voice.

This scene is made up of 6 funeral dirges or laments sung as the
city of Rome goes up in flames in the background. There is a mood
of celebration. Rome, the ancient enemy of the Christians, persecu-
tor of believers, bringer of destruction upon the earth, now has
perished. It might be difficult for us to understand that kind of
attitude; however, we have not gone through the suffering and pain
of persecution which punctuated the existence of the early church.
If you had lost a loved one through the persecutions of Domitian, you
might well rejoice when this part of Revelation was read aloud in the
worship service. Let us now look at the 6 funeral dirges and laments.

The First Funeral Dirge (18:2b-3)

Fallen, fallen, is Babylon the great!
It has become a dwelling place of demons,
a haunt of every foul spirit,
a haunt of every foul and hateful bird;
for all nations have drunk the wine of her impure passion,
and the kings of the earth have committed fornication with her,
and the merchants of the earth have grown rich with the wealth of
     her wantonness.

The flames of Rome can be seen blazing on the lower stage. A voice
pronounces the final judgment and destruction of Rome, "Fallen,
fallen is Babylon the great." The once proud capital city has now
become a haunt for demons, foul spirits, and hateful birds. It must
have been difficult for a prophet like John to write these words for
Rome was still a powerful and mighty capital city of the world. Yet
by faith he could declare God's judgment upon the mighty and the
powerful. John borrows the essence of his doom hymns from prophe-
cies against Babylon in Isaiah 13 and Jeremiah 51 and against Tyre
in Ezekiel 26 and 27. Amos once sang over Israel, "Fallen, no more
to rise is the virgin Israel; forsaken on her land, with none to raise
her up" (Amos 5:2). Isaiah also speaks in similar words about the
capture of Babylon by Cyrus the Great (Isa. 21:9).

John then turns to give the reasons for the fall of Rome. These
reasons we have encountered before in Revelation. The primary
emphasis is placed upon the evil and wicked influence which the city
has had in society. Again, John uses the motif of a cup filled with
wickedness which Rome had shared with other nations. Sexual sins

wickedness which Rome had shared with other nations. Sexual sins and other evils characterized Roman life-style and had been shared with others. Kings and merchants had delighted in the riches of the city but also had been polluted by it.

The Second Funeral Dirge (18:4-8)

> Then I heard another voice from heaven saying,
> "Come out of her, my people,
> lest you take part in her sins,
> lest you share in her plagues,
> for her sins are heaped high as heaven,
> and God has remembered her iniquities.
> Render to her as she herself has rendered,
> and repay her double for her deeds,
> mix a double draught for her in the cup she mixed.
> As she glorified herself and played the wanton,
> so give her a like measure of torment and mourning.
> Since in her heart she says, 'A queen I sit,
> I am no widow, mourning I shall never see,'
> so shall her plagues come in a single day,
> pestilence and mourning and famine,
> and she shall be burned with fire;
> for mighty is the Lord God who judges her."

The second dirge issues a call for the righteous people to come out of Rome that they may not be influenced by her terrible sins or share in her judgment. Jeremiah, the great prophet, once declared, "Flee from the midst of Babylon, and go out of the land of the Chaldeans, and be as he-goats before the flock" (50:8). God can no longer leave unnoticed the sins of Babylon. They are piled up as high as heaven itself. We have seen how God will use the return of Nero and the Parthian kings to punish Rome. She will get exactly what she deserves; as she has been the perpetrator of double crimes, she should receive double punishment. In a single day Rome has become a widow instead of a queen. As a queen she was at the top of society, rejoicing in her splendor and wealth. Now as a widow she mourns in poverty and helplessness. It seems that the change in role had come about overnight or in just one hour. Instead of money and wealth, she will now have pestilence, mourning, and famine and will be consumed with fire.

The Third Funeral Dirge (18:9-10)

This dirge and the next two are based upon Ezekiel 26—28, a hymn of doom for Tyre.

> And the kings of the earth, who committed fornication and were wanton with her, will weep and wail over her when they see the smoke of her burning; they will stand far off, in fear of her torment and say,
>   "Alas! Alas! thou great city,
>   thou mighty city, Babylon!
>   In one hour
>   has thy judgment come."

The first group to appear on the stage is the kings of the earth. They had sent their wealth and tax money to Rome as the great capital city of the earth. In return they received her authority to rule over the people scattered around the area of the Mediterranean Sea. They had been influenced by her fornication and evil, and now they stand a long way off and watch the city burn. They sing a hymn which begins with the cry of an eagle, *ouai*. We have mentioned earlier that often John uses the cry of the eagle to herald bad tidings. *Ouai* pronounced quickly gives the shrieking sound of an eagle which is usually translated woe or alas in our English Bible. The kings do not want to get too close to the burning city for fear they, too, will be destroyed. In their long purple garments, wearing their golden crowns, they stand in graphic contrast to the destruction and terror within the city of Babylon.

The Fourth Funeral Dirge (18:11-17*a*)

> And the merchants of the earth weep and mourn for her, since no one buys their cargo any more, cargo of gold, silver, jewels, and pearls, fine linen, purple, silk and scarlet, all kinds of scented wood, all articles of ivory, all articles of costly wood, bronze, iron, and marble, cinnamon, spice, incense, myrrh, frankincense, wine, oil, fine flour and wheat, cattle and sheep, horses and chariots, and slaves, that is, human souls.
>   "The fruit for which thy soul longed has gone from thee
>   and all thy dainties, thy splendor are lost to thee, never to be
>   found again!"
> The merchants of these wares, who gained wealth from her, will stand far off, in fear of her torment, weeping and mourning aloud,
>   "Alas, alas, for the great city

that was clothed in fine linen, in purple and scarlet,
bedecked with gold, with jewels and with pearls!
In one hour all this wealth had been laid waste."

Rome was a great center of commerce and trade for the whole
Mediterranean world. Great is the sadness of the merchants as they
stand nearby and watch the city go up in flames. The items which
were traded in Rome now are listed, and we can see the vast commercial traffic that existed. Through the Roman port of Ostia commerce
was developed with all the major towns across the Roman world.

India was known for its jewels and pearls, China for its silk and
cinnamon, Africa for its gold and ivory and costly wood, Arabia for
its spice, incense, myrrh, and frankincense, Armenia for its horses,
Israel for its slaves. Merchants of the city grew rich and fat, dressed
themselves in linen, purple, and scarlet, bedecked with gold and
precious stones and pearls. In one hour all the riches of the city
which came from trading had been destroyed. The merchants standing nearby singing their dirge of lament are only concerned for
themselves and the fact that "In one hour all this wealth has been
laid waste."

The Fifth Funeral Dirge (18:17*b*-20)

And all shipmasters and seafaring men, sailors and all those who
trade on the sea, stood far off and cried out as they saw the smoke of
her burning.
"What city was like the great city?"
And they threw dust on their heads as they wept and mourned,
crying out,
"Alas, alas, for the great city,
where all who had ships at sea grew rich by her wealth!
In one hour she has been laid waste.
Rejoice over her, O heaven,
O saints and apostles and prophets,
for God has given judgment for you against her!"

This third group to cross the stage is made up of the seafaring
people of the Roman Empire. We have said previously that Rome
was a great seaport and the port of Ostia saw many ships dock and
depart every day. The major concern of the sailors is the fact that
the great wealth and material gain of the city has been destroyed.
Throughout these hymns we have sensed the great emphasis upon

materialism and what a great role that played in ancient Rome. People who have their life and heart set in materialistic gain can only weep and mourn over the fall of Rome. These sailors threw dust on their head which was a sign of mourning in the ancient world. They too sing the *ouai, ouai* hymns, as they mourn her passing.

Voices then in heaven echo the hymn of sailors (v. 20). There is rejoicing in heaven over the fall of Rome. This part of the hymn no longer reflects the materialism of the sailors, but rather the righteous rejoicing in heaven of the saints, apostles, and prophets, for God's judgment against Babylon has been brought about.

The Sixth Funeral Dirge (18:21-24)

Then a mighty angel took up a stone like a great millstone and threw it into the sea, saying,
"So shall Babylon the great city be thrown down with violence,
    and shall be found no more;
and the sound of harpers and minstrels, flute players and trumpeters,
    shall be heard in thee no more;
and a craftsman of any craft
    shall be found in thee no more;
and the sound of the millstone
    shall be heard in thee no more;
and the light of the lamp
    shall shine in thee no more;
and the voice of bridegroom and bride
    shall be heard in thee no more;
for thy merchants were the great men of the earth,
    and all nations were deceived by thy sorcery.
And in her was found the blood of prophets and of saints,
    and all who have been slain on earth."

The final funeral dirge is sung by a great angel in heaven. A final destruction is brought upon the city as the great millstone is thrown down upon the land ending everyday life in the city. The judgment that Rome had placed upon the martyrs bringing about their death now has been reversed and directed to Rome. She has been sentenced to die. Jeremiah said about Babylon of the Old Testament, "Thou has said concerning this place that thou wilt cut it off, so that nothing shall dwell on it, neither men nor beast, and it shall be desolate for ever" (Jer. 51:62). Just a short while before John had written Revela-

tion, Pompeii had been covered by volcanic ash in AD 79. The eruption of Mount Vesuvius had come as a surprise, and people were
unexpectedly caught in their everyday pursuits. John forsees something like that happening again at the city of Rome. No longer does
one hear music; the flute and the trumpet were used in both religious
and secular music. The everyday sound of grinding corn is no longer
heard. There is no light in the city. The sound of a marriage festival,
music and dancing, has disappeared.

The real indictment against the city, however, appears in verse 24,
"And in her was found the blood of prophets and saints and all who
have been slain on earth." Rome had brought persecution and death
upon the Christians and now the same was being rained down upon
her.

Scene 3

The Third Judgment—Rejoicing in Heaven
and the Marriage Supper of the Lamb (19:1-10)

The music of Act VI continues; however, the funeral dirges give
way to exultation and celebration in the heavenly world. Somber
music which characterized the kings, the merchants, and the sailors,
now echoes in rejoicing music from the heavenly world. The enemy
of God has been destroyed and the heavenly hosts rejoice.

The First Hymn of Rejoicing

After this I heard what seemed to be the loud voice of a great multitude in heaven crying,
"Hallelujah! Salvation and glory and power belong to our God,
for his judgments are true and just;
he has judged the great harlot who corrupted the earth with her
fornication,
and he has avenged on her the blood of his servants" (19:1-2).

This first hymn comes from a great multitude gathered in heaven,
giving praise to God with the ancient Jewish exultation, "Hallelujah." Various attributes are given to God—salvation, glory,
power. The heavenly hosts rejoice for the reason that God's judgments are true and just. Christians on earth have suffered for many
years under the persecutions of the Roman Empire; now God has
brought his judgment upon the great harlot and her corrupting

forces upon the earth. More important, the blood of the Christians
has been revenged. At times in Revelation the choir sings of the
justice of God's judgment: the host by the heavenly Red Sea (15:3),
the martyrs underneath the altar (16:7). No nation can stand in the
way of God's purpose; no nation can stand against the people of God.
God one day will see that justice is done.

The Second Hymn of Rejoicing

And the twenty-four elders and the four living creatures fell down and
worshiped God who is seated on the throne, saying, "Amen. Hallelujah!" And from the throne came a voice crying, "Praise our God,
all you his servants, you who fear him, small and great" (19:4-5).

The twenty-four elders and the four living creatures and the major
choir in our drama now pick up the hymn of exultation. They sing
the words from Psalm 106:48, "Amen! Praise the Lord!" Throughout
Revelation they have sung of the glory, power, and worthiness of
God and the Lamb.

The Third Hymn of Rejoicing

Then I heard what seemed to be the voice of a great multitude, like
the sound of many waters, like the sound of mighty thunderpeals,
crying,
    "Hallelujah! For the Lord our God the Almighty reigns.
    Let us rejoice and exult and give him the glory,
    for the marriage of the Lamb has come,
    and his Bride has made herself ready;
    it was granted her to be clothed with fine linen, bright and pure"—
for the fine linen is the righteous deeds of the saints. And the angel
said to me, "Write this: Blessed are those who are invited to the
marriage supper of the Lamb." And he said to me, "These are true
words of God." Then I fell down at his feet to worship him, but he said
to me, "You must not do that! I am a fellow servant with you and your
brethren who hold the testimony of Jesus. Worship God." For the
testimony of Jesus is the spirit of prophecy (19:6-10).

Rejoicing over the fall of Rome ends with a musical invitation to
the marriage feast of the Lamb. A great multitude sounding like
many waterfalls shouts praise to God. A final object of praise and
rejoicing is the marriage feast of the Lamb which has been prepared
for the righteous. With the destruction of Babylon there emerges the
hope and joy of Christians with the preparation of a kingdom ruled

by God. Throughout the Old Testament, we encounter the idea of Israel as the wife of God. Israel became faithless in that covenant yet the prophets of Israel would once again be betrothed to God. Ezekiel expressed it: "Yet I will remember my covenant with you in the days of your youth, and I will establish with you an everlasting covenant" (16:60). The fulfillment of that betrothal contract lies in the future, however. Revelation 19 brings the fulfillment—the wedding is announced. It is time for the end of the age to join together the people of God with the Lamb. Mark expresses it well: "Truly, I say to you, I shall not drink again of the fruit of the vine until that day when I drink it new in the kingdom of God" (Mark 14:25). The bride has made herself ready, yet the final gift of purity comes from God himself. "It was granted her to be clothed with fine linen, bright and pure" (v. 8).

There are 7 blessings in the Book of Revelation. One of these is found in verse 9; there is a blessing in being invited to the marriage supper of the Lamb. When the Lord returns, which John depicts in Scene 4, the church will be reunited with Christ and the marriage supper will take place. All true Christians are invited to the table. The bride, then, is the church and the wedding dress of the bride is made up of the righteous deeds of the believers. The Jewish people also expected that at the end of the age when the Messiah returned there would be a messianic banquet. The guests would recline at the table with Abraham as the host. These words of God are true words, not just the invitation to the wedding feast, but all the hymns of rejoicing which have been a part of chapter 19. At the conclusion of this rejoicing in heaven, John is told not to fall down to worship the angel that had been speaking to him. John had been so overwhelmed by the rejoicing of the heavenly world that he was tempted to worship the angel messenger that had brought him the revelation. Both the angel and John proclaim the testimony of Jesus.

Earlier in our study we discovered the word *testimony* comes from the Greek word *martus* from which we also get our word *martyr*. To give your testimony meant to stake your life on what you believe. The testimony of Jesus himself undergirds the Christian word and deed. Jesus was faithful to the Revelation of God. It is his testimony which is also found in the word of the Christian prophet. In the

first-century world there were many false prophets, and one had to
test the witness to be sure he was from God.

Scene 4
The Fourth Judgment—The Word of God (19:11-16)

Then I saw heaven opened and behold, a white horse! He who sat upon
it is called Faithful and True, and in righteousness he judges and
makes war. His eyes are like a flame of fire, an on his head are many
diadems; and he has a name inscribed which no one knows but himself. He is clad in a robe dipped in blood, the name by which he is called
is The Word of God. And the armies of heaven, arrayed in fine linen,
white and pure, followed him on white horses. From his mouth issues
a sharp sword with which to smite the nations, and he will rule them
with a rod of iron; he will tread the wine press of the fury of the wrath
of God the Almighty. On his robe and on his thigh he has a name
inscribed, King of kings and Lord of lords.

With the fall of Rome, John expected the return of Jesus Christ
or the *parousia*. The early church lived in expectancy of this end-
time event. John now depicts this glorious return of the Lord in all
of its splendor and excitement. No longer do we have Jesus represented in animal code, a lamb with seven horns and seven eyes. At
his second coming he will return a victorious warrior king, riding a
white horse. John uses all the images and symbols of kingdoms,
wars, and warriors. Christ appears on the white horse as a great
general, his garments dipped in blood. Many Jews expected such a
warrior Messiah or king at the end of the age. John is using a motif
that would have been real to the people in his own day and time.

However, it is clear that the language is symbolic, even as that of
the marriage supper depicted in the previous verses. In Isaiah 63 we
read,

> Who is this that comes from Edom,
>   in crimsoned garments from Bozrah,
> he that is glorious in his apparel,
> marching in the greatness of his strength? . . .
> Why is thy apparel red,
>   and thy garments like his that treads the wine press?
> I have trodden the wine press alone,
>   and from the peoples no one was with me;
> I trod them in my anger
>   and trampled them in my wrath;

> their lifeblood is sprinkled upon my garments,
> and I have stained all my raiment (vv. 1-3).

The phrase, "In a robe dipped in blood" may also refer to sanctification or purification rather than the blood of warfare. When the covenant was established at Mount Sinai, Moses sprinkled the blood of the sacrificial animal upon the people to make them holy as well. It might also be that the blood on his garments symbolized the persecution that has been upon the earth against the people of God. A bloodbath had been brought upon the earth by the Romans, thus the very martyrdom of the saints has been reflected in the clothing of the Lord.

The title given to this rider is "The Word of God." It is very interesting that his title is one of the favorite titles used by John in his writing. It appears in the Gospel of John, 1 John, and here in Revelation. Perhaps it could be John's own secret signature to his work. The rider of the horse is faithful and true in all that he does and says. He judges and makes war with justice. This is a great king, for he has many crowns upon his head. He rules over the whole world. His glory is so great that no one can oppose him. The heavenly army which follows the Messiah is made up of angelic beings and the glorified martyrs. Perhaps John has in mind that the martyrs will participate in the ultimate defeat of Rome. The army will direct its attention against the Parthian kings and hostile nations led by Nero come alive again.

From Psalm 2:9 we learn that he will smash the nations with an iron rod. The sharp sword in his mouth symbolizes his piercing words of judgment once he comes. The Word of God itself will be the only weapon which the Messiah needs. Throughout the Old Testament "mouth like a sharp sword" represents the words of the prophets. Judgment is also symbolized in verse 15 by the phrase "he will tread the wine press of the fury of the wrath of God the Almighty." Throughout Revelation John has used the theme of the cup of God's wrath or the wine press to represent and symbolize judgment. The wine press is the means by which the judgment comes about; the cup of wine motif is actually the judgment.

On the robe which the Messiah wears is inscribed a title, as well as upon his thigh. The title reads, "King of kings and Lord of lords."

In the ancient world often a title would be inscribed on the royal robes worn by the king. Many of the statues of kings which have been excavated show titles written on their thighs. The reference to thigh can also be viewed in terms of a sword which was worn on the thigh. Many swords have been found with royal inscriptions. The whole emphasis with the title is to once again underline the glory and the power of the Messiah.

Scene 5
The Fifth Judgment—The Angel in the Sun (19:17-18)

> Then I saw an angel standing in the sun, and with a loud voice he called to all the birds that fly in midheaven, "Come together for the great supper of God, to eat the flesh of kings, the flesh of captains, the flesh of mighty men, the flesh of horses and their riders, and the flesh of all men, both free and slave, both small and great."

An angel stands in the sun to announce the last battle between good and evil which in Revelation 16:16 John had called the Battle of Armageddon. The birds of prey and vultures symbolize the coming of great destruction of the enemy forces. From the angel's elevated position in the sun, all the birds of prey can see him and hear his message. This feast of the wicked stands in stark contrast to the beautiful marriage supper of the Lamb. The bodies of the dead on the battlefield provide the meal for the beasts of prey. John was using Ezekiel 39:17 for his imagery; he adds to Ezekiel's list of doomed men, "all men, both free and slave, both small and great." The emphasis is that all men opposed to the will of God and enemies of the Christians will be overcome. Even before the battle begins it is obvious that the defeat of the enemy will be great.

Scene 6
The Sixth Judgment—The Battle of Armageddon (19:19-21)

> And I saw the beast and the kings of the earth with their armies gathered to make war against him who sits upon the horse and against his army. And the beast was captured, and with it the false prophet who in its presence had worked the signs by which he deceived those who had received the mark of the beast and those who worshiped its image. These two were thrown alive into the lake of fire that burns with brimstone. And the rest were slain by the sword of him who sits

upon the horse, the sword that issues from his mouth; and all the birds were gorged with their flesh.

Throughout the Book of Revelation we have been building up to this climax, one last battle between good and evil. However, the battle is over before it begins, as John devotes only three verses to the battle itself. The emphasis is placed upon the fact that no force can oppose the Messiah when he returns. Many modern teachers and preachers have stressed and overemphasized the Battle of Armageddon, thinking it the most important event of the Book of Revelation. Yet, for John, there is no real battle because no one can resist the glory of the coming Messiah.

The beasts and the kings of the earth and their armies gather to make war against the returning Messiah; however, no battle is depicted nor described. Immediately in verse 20 the beast is captured and the false prophets with it are thrown alive into the lake of fire that burns with brimstone. The rest of the enemy are slain by the sword of him who sits upon the horse, the sword representing the word of judgment of God. Again, the symbolism of the whole battlefield scene comes before our eyes. Those who oppose him are judged.

Some have tried to make the battle so literal they have even counted the horses in that part of the Middle East, to see if there will be enough for a last battle. Obviously John is depicting a symbolic struggle between good and evil. Although that type of struggle may start with a battle, for John the ultimate emphasis is upon spiritual struggle between Satan and his helpers and the Messiah and his followers. Victory has been prophesied all the way through the book and is quickly achieved at the end of chapter 19.

It is interesting that the last struggle between good and evil is in Act VI, Scene 6, and this number in the code represents evil. Although the word *Armageddon* is not used in chapter 19, we did encounter it in 16:16, describing one last struggle between good and evil. Most interpreters would also attach that name to the battle described in chapter 19. It may be that John had in mind a struggle such as the struggle of Christ with Satan at the cross. The struggle ends in complete victory in the battle depicted in chapter 19.

Scene 7
The Seventh Judgment—Satan Cast into the Abyss (20:1-3)

Then I saw an angel coming down from heaven, holding in his hand the key of the bottomless pit and a great chain. And he seized the dragon, that ancient serpent who is the Devil and Satan, and bound him for a thousand years, and threw him into the pit and shut it and sealed it over him, that he should deceive the nations no more, until the thousand years were ended. After that he must be loosed for a little while.

Scene 7 demonstrates to us that there is no real dualism in Revelation; there is never direct confrontation between the Messiah and Satan. An angel captures Satan and puts him into the abyss, demonstrating the powerlessness of the forces of evil. Earlier we encountered the term abyss in the Book of Revelation as a shaft leading into the interior of the earth where evil or demonic forces were kept. The angel places Satan into this pit, binds him with a chain, and locks him up for a thousand years. The angel also has the key to the pit. A seal is placed upon the pit so that Satan's imprisonment will be complete.

The Jewish people expected a rebellion of chaos, which is often depicted as a monster, against God at the end of the age. The beginning of history featured a struggle between God and chaos, from which he brought forth the earth. This theme worked its way into end-time events and here John is picking up this idea in terms of a struggle between God and the forces of evil. There is a thousand-year period in which the forces of evil will not be present upon the earth. Before the year 100 BC, Judaism believed the messianic kingdom would last forever on our present earth. Later they came to believe that the earth would not be the place for the messianic kingdom and that a temporary manifestation on the present earth would be followed by an eternal place prepared for the completion of the reign of the Messiah. No where else in Jewish literature is the temporary kingdom designated as having one thousand years, 400 is more typical among the Jewish books (see 2 Esdras 7:28). John foresees this thousand-year reign without Satan as an attempt to evangelize the remaining heathen nations. At the end of the thousand years will be one short attempt of Satan to reestablish his domain, but he is quickly destroyed.

Act VI has shown us the implication of the fall of Rome outlined in Act V. Scenes 1 and 2 portrayed a very detailed description of the fall of Rome which would have brought hope and joy to many Christian hearts who have lost loved ones in the persecutions of Caesar Domitian. At the same time, John viewed the fall of Rome as the beginning of the end-time events. Caesar Nero would reappear as an Antichrist figure to lead the Parthian kings from the East and bring about the final struggle that would end the age. John lived in the expectancy that his days were the last days of human history. He lived in the crisis of his own moments of history and gave to those moments an eschatological interpretation. With Rome in flames, the heavens are opened and we see the messianic-banquet table of the Messiah, prepared and ready for the reunion with the bride on earth. In Scene 4 John depicted the glorious arrival of the Messiah leading the heavenly host in a struggle between good and evil which hardly begins before it is over—a victorious achievement for the Messiah! There is no struggle when one confronts him. Satan is defeated and the forces of evil by the Word of God.

In a timeless sense throughout human history the struggle between good and evil will go on. The struggle began at the cross with Christ defeating Satan. Throughout human history there are many such battles of Armageddon; each time we are given the assurance that good will be victorious; no one can resist the power of the Lord. We all look forward with hope to that day when the victory will be completed and our Lord returns with evil ultimately conquered.

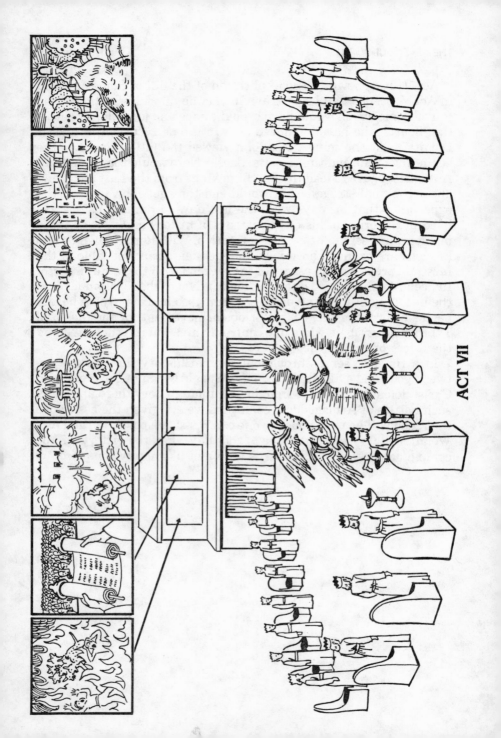

ACT VII

Act VII
The Seven Great Promises

Revelation 20:4 to 22:5

Stage Setting

In the seven windows of the stage building we see seven visions of the promises of God to his people. The act begins with the depiction of the millennium in window 1. Act VII also brings the culmination of world history, and the veil is parted so we might behold things to come, especially the descent of the new Jerusalem. On the lower stage we view the throne of God surrounded by the twenty-four elders and four living creatures. Seven burning torches blaze in front of the throne. The lower stage is separated from the audience by a sea of glass.

The Jewish Temple

In each act of Revelation we have found some emphasis from the Jewish Temple: Seven-branched candlestick, altar of sacrifice, altar of incense, ark of the covenant, closing of the holy of holies, and the whole Temple. Now in the concluding act of Revelation the Temple once again is featured. The new Jerusalem that comes down from heaven in the concluding scene of Revelation is, in essence, the holy of holies of the Temple—it is cubical in shape. The great drama is concluded with the promise that God will be amongst his people, and the Lamb will be the light of the city.

Scene 1
The First Promise—The Millennium (20:4*a*-10)

Then I saw thrones, and seated on them were those to whom judgment was committed. Also I saw the souls of those who had been beheaded for their testimony to Jesus and for the word of God, and who had not worshiped the beast or its image and had not received its mark on their foreheads or their hands. They came to life again and reigned with Christ a thousand years. The rest of the dead did not come to life

127

again until the thousand years were ended. This is the first resurrection. Blessed and holy is he who shares in the first resurrection! Over such the second death has no power, but they shall be priests of God and of Christ, and they shall reign with him a thousand years.

And when the thousand years are ended, Satan will be loosed from his prison and will come out to deceive the nations which are at the four corners of the earth, that is, Gog and Magog, to gather them for battle; their number is like the sand of the sea. And they marched up over the broad earth and surrounded the camp of the saints and the beloved city; but fire came down from heaven and consumed them, and the devil who had deceived them was thrown into the lake of fire and brimstone where the beast and false prophet were, and they will be tormented day and night for ever and ever.

More than any other subject in Revelation, the millennium is hotly debated. John sets forth as his first great promise a thousand-year reign of Christ. The debate rages over where the reign will be and whether or not it should be viewed as symbolic or as literal. We have invited three guests to present their views on the millennium; these three guests represent the three major schools of thought on the subject.

First of all, we would like you to meet Dr. B. H. Postmillennialist.

DR. B. H. POSTMILLENNIALIST: I am very happy to be with you. I would like to give you a basic summary of my views concerning the millennium. Postmillennialists believe that there will be some signs of the end of the age, the first the return of Israel to the Holy Land, the second, increasing improvement of the world. It is obvious that one of these signs has already taken place; in 1947 Israel returned to the land. I believe also that it is obvious the world is improving. Just for a moment consider all of the great and good things that have happened since the turn of the century in 1900. This generation has witnessed more great accomplishments than all generations that lived before. Since 1900 the airplane has been invented, automobiles have come into existence, electricity has brought an age of comfort to the world, and, above all, new medicines and medical services have appeared on the scene. There have been more inventions for good in these last eighty years than all the years previous in man's history.

It is evident that we will slowly merge into the so-called millennium or one-thousand-year reign of Christ. However, Christ will not be on earth, but will remain in heaven and work through his church here on earth. The church will grow stronger and spread across the face of the earth until suddenly Christians will realize that they are in the millennium. Evil will recede or no longer be a significant force. I really believe that perhaps the millennium started in 1947 when the Jewish people returned to their homeland. During these first few years of the millennium it is necessary to eradicate a few remaining parts of evil, including a few wars. However, it is to be underlined that no major war has been fought since World War II. The millennium will continue to develop and show the strength of the church. Toward the end of the thousand-year reign, the church will take its strength for granted and Christ will have to intervene in the world. Then will come the end of the age with judgment and heaven or hell.

Thank you, Dr. B. H. Postmillennialist.
Our second guest is Dr. Hal Premillennialist.

DR. HAL PREMILLENNIALIST: It is good to be with you today. I would like to set forth my view of the millennium. There are many different kinds of premillennialists; it is one of the oldest ways of looking at the Book of Revelation. Many of the early church fathers took a historical premillennialist view of the Scriptures. In essence, Christ will return before the thousand-year reign begins and will be here on earth for a literal one-thousand-year reign.

About one hundred years ago, a new school of thought came into being under the premillennialists heading called dispensationalism. It was founded by Miss Margaret McDonald of Scotland, who belonged to the Plymouth Brethren Church. It was revealed to her one day while speaking in tongues that there would be an extra coming of Christ called the rapture and, in addition, four resurrections and five judgments. Her pastor, Dr. John N. Darby, happened to visit with Miss McDonald and copied down her revelations, which became the foundation of Dispensationalism. Dr. C. I. Scofield used many of Darby's ideas in his *Scofield Bible* notes.

Let me explain this rather complicated view of premillennialism. We believe the world will become increasingly evil; we do agree with the postmillennialist brothers that Israel returning to the homeland is a sign of the end of the age. The Lord will intervene in what we call a rapture coming. The purpose of this coming is to take the church, the Holy Spirit, and all of the church-age saints who have passed out of this world. Following the rapture of Christ there will be a seven-year period of great tribulation. We divide this into three and one-half-year periods.

In the first three and one-half years, Israel will be allowed to rebuild the Temple in the Holy Land. There will also be a resurgence of ten nations which many believe will be the common market nations. They will rule the world with Italy as the number 1 nation. In the second three and one-half-year period these ten nations will turn against Israel and many of the plagues pointed out in the Book of Revelation will fall upon Israel. During that period there will be 144,000 Jewish evangelists who will bring the gospel to the world, and many will believe. At the end of the seven-year period of tribulation Christ will intervene and return to the earth to set up the thousand-year reign. Nations will be judged to see which nations will participate in the thousand-year reign; this we call the sheep and goats' judgment. At the end of the thousand-year reign there will also be a resurrection of the evil people and they will be judged. In our system, then we have three comings of Christ, his birth, rapture, and end-time coming.

There are four resurrections:

1. The *harvest resurrection* at the rapture, Old Testament saints and church-age saints

2. *The gleanings,* those who died during the seven-year tribulation

3. Those who died during the millennium

4. The resurrection of the evil

There are five judgments:

1. Believer's sin judged at Calvary

2. Believer's works judged at the judgment seat after the rapture

3. Jews judged by persecution during the tribulation

4. The nations judged at the millennium

5. Judgment upon evil, the great white throne judgment

Our system is very complicated. Our charts and graphs will help you understand the system.

Thank you, Dr. Hal Premillennialist.
Our last guest is Dr. Edgar Amillennialist.

DR. EDGAR AMILLENNIALIST: Good day. It is good to be here with you today. I think after hearing these first two guests you will be persuaded that the best approach is a symbolic approach. My view is that the millennium is a thousand-year reign of Christ in a symbolic sense. One thousand is based upon the number ten; in the number code of apocalyptic literature ten means completeness. This reign of Christ started at the cross where Satan was overwhelmed and defeated by Christ. In one sense we might call that the Battle of Armageddon. Christ has been reigning since the cross and will reign until the end of the age. No one can predict the exact day of the end nor how long this reign will be. In one sense Satan is locked and chained up; he no longer has the power that he had before the crucifixion. Thus, we are in the millennium and Christ is reigning.

We would like to thank our 3 guests for being with us today. From these 3 interviews it is evident that there is very little agreement about the thousand year reign of Christ. It is tragic that so much emphasis has been put upon the subject of the millennium; it has become an obstacle to the study of Revelation in many of our churches. Many pastors will not preach from Revelation because of all the confusion on the subject. There are so many positive verses within the book that need to be heard. So often so much theological baggage is brought to these three verses that they become a center of controversy among us. Let us allow these verses to speak for themselves and examine what John is saying apart from all the various schools of thought. It is most surprising that so little space is given to the millennium. We discovered that nearly 2 chapters were devoted to the fall of Rome. Only 3 verses are given to the millennium.

In a similar pattern to Daniel 7:9ff, John beholds a throne placed in heaven. In Daniel 7:22 we are told that when the ancient of days came the judgment was given to the saints and these saints would

receive the kingdom. John declares that the saints will reign with
Christ. Immediately the martyrs are singled out to be preeminent in
this rule. "Also I saw the souls of those who had been beheaded for
their testimony to Jesus and for the word of God, and who had not
worshiped the beast or its image and had not received its mark on
their foreheads or their hands" (Rev. 20:4a).

In Revelation the martyrs have played a very significant role. In
chapter 6 they were given a special place under the altar in heaven.
It would be very important for John to reassure those who had lost
loved ones and who themselves might be facing death that a special
place of honor will be given to those who had been beheaded because
of their testimony for Christ. The martyrs were those who had resisted the beast—Rome, even to the point of death. They refused to
accept its mark and even allowed their families to starve rather than
be tattooed with the face of Caesar. Thus the martyrs are singled out
for special praise even as a larger company of saints is indicated in
verse 4a. All true Christian believers "came to life again and reigned
with Christ a thousand years." The larger company of Christians, as
well as the martyrs, will reign with Christ for a thousand years.

John then speaks of 2 resurrections: the first, the resurrection of
the saints and the martyrs, and a second resurrection following the
thousand year reign. Many questions remain unanswered. We are
not told precisely that Christ is on the earth during the one thousand
year period of time. In Jewish literature there are many different
views of the reign of the Messiah. Rabbi Akibi believed the reign
would be as long as Israel sojourned in the wilderness or forty years.
Rabbi Jehuda thought it would be four thousand years. Rabbi Jose,
the Galilean, set forth sixty years. John seems to be taking most of
his information from Ezekiel 36:7 where we find mention of a return
of Israel and the restoration of the nation under the rule of a new
David. Following that unspecified period of time there is a rebellion
of Gog and Magog and then a promise of a new Jerusalem with a new
Temple and kingdom to come (Ezek. 40—48).

It is evident that we do not have enough information to write a
theology of the millennium nor develop any great school of thought.
Perhaps the country preacher was right after all when on being
asked about which view of the millennium he took, he answered, "I
am a Panmillennialist; it is all going to pan out in the end anyway,

why worry about it." Baptists have traditionally not taken a stand on the millennium but have emphasized the second coming or return of Jesus Christ. It is evident that Christ is ruling in our world and one day he will return. God will take care of all the details.

John sets forth one last struggle of evil in the battle of Gog and Magog. Following the thousand year reign, Satan will be released from prison and gather the nations together for this final battle. Gog and Magog were ancient kingdoms north of Israel. Their names are found as early as the Tell el Amarna tablets. In Ezekiel, we find the expectation that some northern nation will come against the people of God and attack Jerusalem. Gog and Magog are symbolic of the enemies of God, represented here by the northern powers. Thus it is foolish to try to locate modern nations such as Russia or China in reference to the fulfillment of these words. John is telling us that God's enemies will continue their rebellion until the very last day. The assurances and promises are that God's enemies will be destroyed and the devil will be thrown into the lake of fire and brimstone forever and ever.

Scene 2
The Second Promise—The Judgment of Evil (20:11-15)

Then I saw a great white throne and him who sat upon it; from his presence earth and sky fled away, and no place was found for them. And I saw the dead, great and small, standing before the throne, and books were opened. Also another book was opened, which was the book of life. And the dead were judged by what was written in the books, by what they had done. The sea gave up the dead in it, Death and Hades gave up the dead in them, and all were judged by what they had done. Then Death and Hades were thrown into the lake of fire. This is the second death, the lake of fire; and if any one's name was not found written in the book of life, he was thrown into the lake of fire.

From Revelation 20:4-6 we are led to expect a second resurrection; some scholars believe that those who appear before the Great White Throne judgment of God will be the evil who are brought to life at the second resurrection. However, it is evident that the judgment is more inclusive than that; all must stand before the judgment bar of God. Thus Scene 2 symbolizes the great judgment of God. Books are opened, including the Book of Life, which theme comes from ancient Persia where tax-paying citizens were listed in a book of life. Jewish people in exile took over the idea and gave to it the thought that God maintained such a list; that God also listed the good deeds and bad deeds of mankind. The Book of Life, however, contains a special list of all of those who belong to the Lamb. These have a special place in the sight of God. The new Jerusalem is a place designed for them. Those whose names are not found in the Book of Life are judged and put into the lake of fire. "If any one's name was not found written in the book of life, he was thrown into the lake of fire" (v. 15). Judgment will be so universal that John reminds us that even those who have been lost at sea will also be brought before his throne. Death and Hades are thrown into the lake of fire. God's victory now is complete and nothing can withstand his marvelous and wonderful reign.

It is interesting that the word *gehenna* translated *hell* is not mentioned in the Book of Revelation. John prefers to use the words *lake of fire*. Throughout Revelation the sea has been a fearful place. The Jewish people thought of an underground sea that had never been conquered by God that was ruled over the evil spirits. Perhaps we need something of this background in the sea of fire.

Scene 3
The Third Promise—The New Heaven and Earth (21:1-3)

Then I saw a new heaven and a new earth; for the first heaven and the first earth had passed away, and the sea was no more. And I saw the holy city, new Jerusalem, coming down out of heaven from God, prepared as a bride adorned for her husband; and I heard a great voice from the throne saying, "Behold, the dwelling of God is with men. He will dwell with them, and they shall be his people, and God himself will be with them."

In the third promise John tells us that the old earth and the old heaven will pass away. The appearance of the Holy City, the new Jerusalem, dominates central stage. In the past, earth and heaven had been separate places; because of sin mankind has been separated from God. John now perceives that God and his people will dwell together in the new age. Heaven and earth will be joined; the new Jerusalem will be the holy of holies itself, descending from heaven, to a new earth which God will create for his people. Thus, the promise is declared, "Behold the dwelling of God is with men. He will dwell with them, and they shall be his people, and God, himself, will be with them." In the background looms Isaiah 65:17 where the great prophet of the Old Testament told of a renewal of the present world. In this new creation there will be no more sea; that would have brought great hope to the Jewish writer who feared the sea. In addition, the sea throughout Revelation has symbolized evil that will be conquered at the end of the age by God.

Thus, in this new world there will be no evil; God's reign will be complete. The whole scene symbolizes the great truth that God will dwell with his people who have experienced the redemption by Christ. "Therefore, if any one is in Christ, he is a new creation; the old has passed away, behold, the new has come" (2 Cor. 6:17). John puts that truth into graphic form by the appearance of the new Jerusalem. However, if one gets too involved in a literalistic interpretation of the city one misses the greater spiritual truth of God dwelling with his people and the new creation to be experienced. More important than the glamour and beauty of the city is the fact that there is no longer a barrier between God and man. There is no longer a separate heaven and earth; there is one dwelling place where man once again can be with God, even as Adam and Eve walked in the garden with their Lord.

Scene 4
The Fourth Promise—Assurance for Believers (21:4-8)

"He will wipe away every tear from their eyes, and death shall be no more, neither shall there be mourning nor crying or pain any more, for the former things have passed away." And he who sat upon the throne said, "Behold, I make all things new." Also he said, "Write this, for these words are trustworthy and true." He said to me, "It is done! I am the Alpha and Omega, the beginning and the end. To the thirsty I will give water without price from the fountain of the water of life. He who conquers shall have this heritage and I will be his God and he shall be my son. But as for the cowardly, the faithless, the polluted, as for murderers, fornicators, sorcerers, idolators, and all liars, their lot shall be in the lake that burns with fire and brimstone, which is the second death."

Christians are now given another great promise, that the painful experiences of this world will not be a part of the new world. We have been told that God will abide with his people. Thus there cannot be pain and death in his presence. Earlier in 7:17 the martyrs were told that God would wipe the tears from their eyes. In Isaiah 25:8 we read the words, "He will swallow up death for ever, and the Lord God will wipe away tears from all faces, and the reproach of his people he will take away from all the earth, for the Lord has spoken." John sees these words of Isaiah fulfilled in the new Jerusalem where God will dwell with his people.

God now speaks directly for the first time since the opening chapters of the Book of Revelation. "Behold, I make all things new." This new creation now has cosmic significance. God is the beginning of all things and the end, the Alpha and the Omega. We also see in these words the fulfillment of the Beatitudes of the Sermon on the Mount. The mourners will be comforted and those who search after righteousness given this water of life. The persecuted or those who conquer will enter into the kingdom of God. However, the greatest of all promises is found in the words, "I will be his God and he shall be my son" (v. 7).

Even as John beholds the blessing of the world to come, he also takes time out to look over his shoulder into the lake of fire. We encounter a long list of those who are not in the presence of God. It is very interesting that at the top of the list of those in the lake of fire are the cowards. For John cowardliness was indeed a very important sin. Those who now stand with God in the heavenly world are those who have overcome persecution, who were not afraid to meet death. Those who surrendered their faith and gave in to the persecution of Domitian are now in the lake of fire.

All the others listed also are in some way related to the evil and sin of Satan and his 2 helper beasts. The word "polluted" in verse 8 would refer to the obscenities involved in cursing the name of Christ and saying "Caesar is Lord." The murderers would be those who had put to death the martyrs and the very people of God. Fornicators, sorcerers, and idolators are groups of people all involved in the worship of Caesar's statue. Liars are those who have worshiped the beast and denied the truth of God. Those who chose to reside in Babylon now are the ones who die in the fire and brimstone of the lake of fire. Those who chose to overcome now shall dwell in the new Jerusalem.

These words would have brought great hope to the people living in Ephesus, Pergamum, Thyratira, and other cities. These Christians had lost loved ones to the persecution of Rome. Now they can look across time and behold what the new creation will bring them in terms of blessing. They can also see that evil will not persevere. Those who have turned their face toward Jesus will also one day receive their just due. This would have brought great hope and expectation to their hearts.

Scene 5
The Fifth Promise—The New Jerusalem (21:9-21)

Then came one of the seven angels who had the seven bowls full of the seven last plagues, and spoke to me, saying, "Come, I will show you the Bride, the wife of the Lamb." And in the Spirit he carried me away to a great, high mountain, and showed me the holy city Jerusalem coming down out of heaven from God, having the glory of God, radiant like a most rare jewel, like a jasper, clear as crystal. It had a great, high wall, with twelve gates, and at the gates twelve angels, and on the gates the names of the twelve tribes of the sons of Israel were inscribed; on the east three gates, on the north three gates, on the south three gates, and on the west three gates. And the wall of the city had twelve foundations, and on them twelve names of the twelve apostles of the Lamb.

And he who talked to me had a measuring rod of gold to measure the city and its gates and walls. The city lies foursquare, its length the same as its breadth; and he measured the city with his rod, twelve thousand stadia; its length and breadth and height are equal. He also measured its wall, one hundred and forty-four cubits by a man's measure, that is, an angel's. The wall was built of jasper while the city was pure gold, clear as glass. The foundations of the wall of the city were adorned with every jewel; the first was jasper, the second sapphire, the third agate, the fourth emerald, the fifth onyx, the sixth carnelian, the seventh chrysolite, the eighth beryl, the ninth topaz, the tenth chrysoprase, the eleventh jacinth, the twelfth amethyst. And the twelve gates were twelve pearls, each of the gates made of a single pearl, and the street of the city was pure gold, transparent as glass.

John sees as the spiritual capital of this new creation the holy of holies itself, the new Jerusalem, descending from heaven, cubical in shape. "The city lies foursquare, its length the same as its breadth; and he measured the city with his rod, twelve thousand stadia; its length and breadth and height are equal." It was so incredibly beautiful that John could not express it in prose and chose poetry to do so. John selects the beauty of precious jewels to express the unusual nature of the Holy City. One should not take this in a literal sense and make the new Jerusalem into something quite materialistic. We are dealing here with something spiritual.

The city itself has the appearance of a jasper. God himself had been described in the very same terms in 4:3. "And he who sat there appeared like jasper." Thus the city itself is the very presence of God. John goes on then to describe the city in some detail. It is very similar to the city that Ezekiel saw in his vision, Ezekiel 48:30ff; the 12 gates of the city stand open so that the people may go out to possess their land. Here in John's vision there are 12 gates that stand open so that the nations of the world may come into the Holy City.

First Enoch 33—36 also speaks of the 12 gates of heaven, 3 at each point of the compass. The ancient world of astrology also spoke of 12 signs of the zodiac, these as the gates by which the sun, moon, and the planets entered onto their courses. Thus, there is a rich field of background for the idea of 12 gates of the heavenly Jerusalem.

Here in Revelation the listing of the gates is somewhat unusual, east, north, south, and west. One also finds that unusual listing in Ezekiel 42:16-19. Scholars have viewed this as an attempt by John to combat the usual listing of the zodiacal cycle. The city is surrounded by a wall which is 144 cubits; in the number code of Revelation 144 is based on the number 12 and signifies wholeness. The emphasis, then, is upon the security and wholeness of the city.

The size of the city is 12,000 stadia by 12,000 stadia; again the emphasis is upon the number 12, signifying wholeness. The numbers should not be taken literally as in some English translations which translate the 12,000 stadia with 1,500 miles by 1,500 miles. The whole significance of the coded number is lost in this. The city will be large enough for everyone. In John 14:2 Jesus said something similar: "In my Father's house are many rooms." The wall is built from jasper which again would indicate the presence of God. The whole city is made out of crystal, clear as glass. It's main street is also made of transparent gold. Again we can see the symbolism involved, for no one has ever seen gold clear as glass. John is straining with words to capture the beauty of a spiritual place.

John now describes the 12 foundation stones underneath the city.

In the Old Testament there were 12 precious stones on the breast-plate of the high priest. In addition, in the world of astrology these 12 precious stones were connected with the 12 signs of the zodiac. However, here John reverses the listing of the stones as found in astrology to once again make his case against those involved with astrology. The following list will show that John has reversed the signs of the zodiac. The following is the usual listing of signs with stones: (1) The ram, amethyst, (2) the bull, jacinth, (3) the twins, chrysoprase, (4) the crab, topaz, (5) the lion, beryl, (6) the virgin, chrysolite, (7) the scales, carnelian, (8) the scorpion, onyx, (9) the archer, emerald, (10) the goat, agate, (11) the water carrier, sapphire, (12) the fishes, jasper. The order in Revelation is the exact opposite of this list.

John now describes the 12 gates of the city with each one being made from a single pearl. In the Talmud Rabbi Johanan related that the gates of Jerusalem would be made out of pearls, measuring 30 cubits by 30. John next tells us that the street of the city is made of pure gold. Perhaps John had in mind the great Milky Way sweeping across the heavens. The beauty of the city in every respect points to the love of God for his people and his presence among them. No human words are sufficient to express John's vision. It will always be more startling and extensive than we can comprehend.

Scene 6
The Sixth Promise—The City's Illumination (21:22-27)

And I saw no temple in the city, for its temple is the Lord God the Almighty and the Lamb. The city has no need of sun or moon to shine upon it, for the glory of God is its light and its lamp is the Lamb. By its light shall the nations walk; and the kings of the earth shall bring their glory into it, and its gates shall never be shut by day—and there shall be no night there; they shall bring into it the glory and the honor of the nations. But nothing unclean shall enter it, nor anyone who practices abomination of falsehood, only those who are written in the Lamb's book of life.

In the new city there is no need for a temple; the city itself is the holy of holies, and God's presence is in its midst. Everyone there has a close relationship with him; there is no need for a separate temple. All those who dwell in the city are in the holy of holies. God is the

Isaiah 42-2

very light of the city; there is no need for the sun or moon. John then promises that all the nations will no longer be deceived by Satan but will turn and bring their riches to the Holy City. To the Christians living in the seven churches it appeared as if the nations were under the control of the Antichrist and his forces. They were being used to bring persecution upon the followers of God. But now in this new order God will be in control of all things.

George Caird has said it well: "Nothing from the old order which has value in the sight of God is debarred from entry into the new." Some have projected theories that these verses seem out of place here and perhaps they were originally in connection with the description of the millennium in chapter 20. Yet if one reads the total content, one realizes that the verses do relate well to what John has said about God being in control of all things and his power reigning supreme over the new earth. There is no need for the gates to be shut for no unclean person nor those who have committed abomination will be in the city; they are in the lake of fire. Only those who have been written in the Lamb's Book of Life will be a part of this Holy City.

Scene 7
The Seventh Promise—The River of Life (22:1-5)

Then he showed me the river of the water of life, bright as crystal, flowing from the throne of God and of the Lamb through the middle of the street of the city; also, on either side of the river, the tree of life with its twelve kinds of fruit, yielding its fruit each month; and the leaves of the tree were for the healing of the nations. There shall no more be anything accursed, but the throne of God and of the Lamb shall be in it, and his servants shall worship him; they shall see his face, and his name shall be on their foreheads. And night shall be no more; they need no light of lamp or sun for the Lord God will be their light, and they shall reign forever and ever.

The Bible begins with a beautiful garden with fruit trees and ends with a similar picture here in Revelation. John moves from the motif of the city to that of the garden, punctuated with the beautiful river of the water of life. The image of the throne appears in every chapter of the Book of Revelation except two, and here it appears as the source for the river of life. The river also was important in the Garden of Eden (Gen. 2:9ff.)

Ezekiel 47:9 also spoke of a river in his vision of the new temple. John indicates that on either side of the river there are trees of life. There is some debate over the translation of verse 2 in reference to where these trees are located. However, the Revised Standard Version text seems to have the best translation of a series of trees on both sides of the river. Ezekiel also describes a similar picture: "And on the banks, of both sides of the river, there will grow all kinds of trees for food. Their leaves will not wither nor their fruit fail, but they will bear fresh fruit every month, because the water for them flows from the sanctuary. Their fruit will be for food, and their leaves for healing," (Ezek. 47:12). John seems to have the same thing in mind as Ezekiel. The leaves of the trees of life will be used for the healing of the nations. In a symbolic sense there will be no pain, nor sickness, nor sorrow in this city because of God's presence; even the leaves of the trees will manifest that.

The picture is also painted of all the saints worshiping God throughout the ages. Worship has played a big role in Revelation through all the acts; it is only fitting that in the final act the drama should conclude with those saints who have overcome worshiping the living God who is the light of the city. John declares, "They shall reign for ever and ever."

Act VII has identified the seven great promises given to the saints and has presented a new creation, a new world like God intended for this earth to be from the beginning. It is a place of rivers and trees, a place of supreme beauty. There is a promise of the reign of Christ and the assurance of the presence of God in the midst of his people. No more separation will exist between God and man. It is a vision of supreme happiness for those who have followed the Lamb. Ultimately Act VII brings us the final triumph of God in the world and in the universe. In response to these visions, one can only fall and worship God even as the saints have done throughout eternity.

Epilogue

Revelation 22:6-21

And he said to me, "These words are trustworthy and true. And the Lord, the God of the spirits of the prophets has sent his angel to show his servants what must soon take place. And behold, I am coming soon."

Blessed is he who keeps the words of the prophecy of this book.

I, John, am he who heard and saw these things. When I heard and saw them, I fell down to worship at the feet of the angel who showed them to me; but he said to me, "You must not do that! I am a fellow servant with you and your brethren the prophets, with those who keep the words of this book. Worship God."

And he said to me, "Do not seal up the words of the prophecy of this book, for the time is near. Let the evildoer still do evil and the filthy still be filthy, and the righteous still do right, and the holy still be holy."

"Behold I am coming soon, bringing my recompense, to repay every one for what he has done. I am the Alpha and the Omega, the first and the last, the beginning and the end."

Blessed are those who wash their robes, that they may have the right to the tree of life and they may enter the city by the gates. Outside are the dogs and sorcerers and fornicators and murderers and idolators and every one who loves and practices falsehood.

"I, Jesus, have sent my angel to you with this testimony for the churches. I am the root and the offspring of David, the bright morning star."

The Spirit and the Bride say, "Come." And let him who hears say "Come." And let him who is thirsty come, let him who desires take the water of life without price.

I warn every one who hears the words of the prophecy of this book: if any one adds to them, God will add to him the plagues described in this book and if any one takes away from the words of the book of this prophecy, God will take away his share in the tree of life and in the holy city, which are described in this book.

He who testifies to these things says, "Surely I am coming soon." Amen. Come, Lord Jesus! The grace of the Lord Jesus be with all the saints. Amen.

At the conclusion of Greek tragic drama, one main character on the ledge of the stage would give the final epilogue. John performs this task in 22:6-21. Following that, the choir leaves the main stage through the exodus and the drama is over.

The heavenly angel makes one final declaration to John upon the trustworthiness of the words that have been given to him. From the very beginning of Revelation stress has been placed upon the witness and the return of the Lord. This same spirit that had been with the Old Testament prophets has also been with John. He, too, is a prophet, one who declares the truth of God to his people. The final blessing of the seven blessings in Revelation is bestowed upon those who keep the prophecy of the Book of Revelation.

In verse 8, John begins his final monologue, "I, John, am he who heard and saw these things." Again, John falls down before the angel as if to worship him and is reminded once again as in 19:10 that he should not do that. The words of the angel in response to John's actions emphasize the authority of John and his role as prophet, "You must not do that! I am a fellow servant with you and your brethren the prophets and with those who keep the words of this book." These words "your brethren the prophets" seem to include John in the prophet's ranks. They are a divine seal of approval on the Revelation of John and his testimony to God. God alone is to receive the worship of mankind.

In the Old Testament, Samuel spoke of the words of God being shut off until the wicked become even more wicked, (2 Sam. 12:9). John foresees this time as having come, "Let the evildoers still do evil, and the filthy still be filthy" (22:11). These words were designed for the end-time generation, and now that time has come. Enoch was also told that his visions were "Not for this generation, but for a remote one yet to come" (1 Enoch 1:2). Then the voice of Christ is then heard announcing, "I am coming soon" (22:20). He will bring with him his reward, and we have seen the greatest reward of all is access to God in the Holy City.

The Lord holds before the believers of all the churches the promise that if they persevere and overcome the gates will be open to the Holy City. They too must wash their robes in the blood of the lamb, even as the martyrs before them have given the ultimate sacrifice and have gone on into the city. Again we are reminded that outside

the city are the evil persons; they will not have a part in the fellowship with God. Such words as *sorcerers, fornicators,* and *murderers*
are used once again. They have resisted God throughout this age,
and they will not have a part in the Holy City but rather be in the
lake of fire.

All that John has said and declared has been given to him by the
angelic messenger. Christ makes a final declaration that he is the
root of David's line and the very foundation of the whole royal line.
He also declares to be the bright and morning star; thus we have a
fulfillment of Numbers 24:17 that a star shall come forth from Jacob;
Jesus Christ is that star and the ruler of the age.

The choir now files from the lower stage through the exodus out
of the theater. As they leave they sing: "The Spirit and the Bride say,
'Come.' Let him who hears say, 'Come.' Let him who is thirsty come,
let him who desires take the water of life without price" (22:17). The
hymn of the choir stresses the availability of salvation for all who
hear the words of John. It is a call for the Christians to persevere
and join that group that sings before God's throne.

The concluding words of John (Rev. 22:18-19) formulate a warning
that no one should add or take away from the words of his book. Such
warnings are also found in other apocalyptic works because of the
use of coded language. It was very important that no words be taken
away from the message. Often in the ancient world when books were
copied by hand and passed on, scribes would change the words of the
original writer, adding their own meanings and distortions. John
feels so strongly at this point that he adds a very strong curse upon
anyone who would change the words, "If any one takes away from
the words of the book of this prophecy, God will take away his share
in the tree of life and the holy city, which are described in this book."
John leaves the stage as the risen Lord makes one final declaration,
"Surely I am coming soon." The choir offstage declares, "Amen.
Come, Lord Jesus."

We have thus seen Revelation as a seven-act drama. It represents
an innovative adaptation of Greek tragic drama. Its dramatic adaptation accounts for striking differences from other so-called apocalyptic books. The writer was not able to express his vision in ordinary
prose; he needed a dramatic medium. The timeless poetic form of

tragedy was well suited to capture his cosmic vision of another world, yet the cyclical nature of Greek history found in Greek tragedy is transformed by him into a prophetic, goal-oriented view of history. The wedding of the timeless and prophetic in Revelation presents us with a spiral theme of history, movement in half-circles toward the end goal.

Many recent studies have demonstrated how the dramatic form of Revelation was used in early Christian liturgy and festivity. Drama and divine worship were closely related in the minds of the first-century Greek world. The Greek tragedy was a medium well known in Asia Minor and particularly in Ephesus as the theater in that great city with its unique seven windows had been both a landmark and a cultural center. Only in that setting can the unique genre of Revelation be understood. Indeed, it is a true syncretistic method of bringing together the Greek and Hebraic worlds, the theater and Temple, cult and drama. The dramatic genre also allows the book to capture the imagination of modern readers. The approach has great possibilities in teaching Revelation in the local church. This dramatic medium has the power to grasp an individual where he or she is and confront him or her with the prophetic message. We are already participating in the power of God's rule and in that power we can be victorious over all the dehumanizing evil powers of our world. On the last page of the book stands the triumphant Lamb, not Caesar, not any "ism."

Revelation Drama Script

Directions for Staging

The typical American stage can easily be adapted to represent the ancient stage at Ephesus. A plywood structure with seven windows (*thuramata*) should be placed across the main stage. Each window should be covered with two-way paper so that a rearview slide projector may be used behind them. This structure should be set back from the edge of the stage to allow a ten-foot ramp across the front of the stage for John and other actors (*proskene*). Below the stage on the main floor of the auditorium, a circular area should be designated for twenty-four choir members and twenty-four small thrones. In the center of the choir should be a larger throne for God. The chorus area should be surrounded by soft blue lights representing the sea of glass. No attempt should be made to depict God on the throne but rather have one bright light behind the throne. The twenty-four choir members should be dressed in white choir robes, with gold crowns on their heads and small harps in their hands. The choir comes into place in the Prologue and remains there for all seven acts.

Room should be left in the back of the chorus level to represent the various themes from the Jewish Temple. In Act I, a large seven-branched menorah should be behind the choir and up against the base of the stage. In Act II, the menorah should be replaced with an altar of sacrifice. In Act III, the altar of sacrifice should be removed and an altar of incense inserted. In Act IV, the altar of incense should be replaced with the ark of the covenant. In Act V, the ark should be removed and smoke should come up from the base of the stage representing the closing of the holy of holies. In Acts VI and VII, the whole stage represents the Temple.

Throughout the drama, great use is made of banners. These can be made of silk or cardboard. The characters can be painted on them. These banners should be attached to wooden poles so that they can be carried across the stage.

Slides to be projected into the windows of the stage can be made by searching through art books and magazines. There are many great art masterworks painted from Revelation.

Music can be adapted from current church music. At other times the choir can chant the biblical text.

Prologue
(Rev. 1:1-8)

Characters: JOHN, CHOIR, SON OF MAN

STAGE SETTING: A dim amber spot comes up on the *proskene* where JOHN stands reading an open scroll.

JOHN (*in a loud voice*): This is the revelation of Jesus Christ, which God gave me to show to his servants what must soon take place; and he made it known by sending his angel to me, his servant John, who bore witness to the word of God and to the testimony of Jesus Christ, even to all that I saw. Blessed is he that reads aloud the words of the prophecy, and blessed are those who hear, and who keep what is written therein; for the time is near.

(*The paintings of the seven cities appear in the seven* thuromata *of the Ephesian stage.*)

JOHN (*in an authoritative voice*): John to the seven churches that are in Asia. Grace to you and peace from him who is and who was and who is to come, and from the seven spirits who are before his throne, and from Jesus Christ the faithful witness, the first-born of the dead, and the ruler of kings on earth.

CHOIR (*entering through the* parados *on either side of the stage building and chanting*): To him who loves us and has freed us from our sins by his blood and made us a kingdom, priests to his God and Father, to him be glory and dominion for ever and ever. Amen. Behold, he is coming with the clouds, and every eye will see him, every one who pierced him; and all tribes of the earth will wail on account of him. Even so. Amen.

(*The* SON OF MAN *enters the* proskene *dressed in a long white robe with a golden girdle about his chest. From his mouth a sharp sword emerges. He has white hair and bronze feet. He declares*)

SON OF MAN: I am the Alpha and the Omega, who is and who was and who is to come, the Almighty.

Act I
The Seven Golden Lampstands
(Rev. 1:9 to 3:22)

Characters: JOHN, SON OF MAN, CHORUS, VOICE OFFSTAGE

STAGE SETTING: The seven paintings of the cities of Asia Minor remain in

the *thuromata*. Seven menorahs (about 5 feet tall), one in each window, should be in their proper place. The SON OF MAN and JOHN, remain on the ledge (*proskene*). The SON OF MAN goes to window 1 and lights the seven candles in the first menorah in sequence with the reading of the seven major points of the letter to Ephesus. Each subsequent letter receives the same treatment.
(*Spotlight on* JOHN)

JOHN: I, John, your brother, who share with you in Jesus the tribulation and the kingdom and the patient endurance, was on the island called Patmos on account of the word of God and the testimony of Jesus. I was in the Spirit on the Lord's day, and I heard behind me a loud voice like a trumpet.

SON OF MAN: Write what you see in a book and send it to the seven churches, to Ephesus and to Smyrna and to Pergamum and to Thyatira and to Sardis and to Philadelphia and to Laodicea.

JOHN (*spotlight moves from* SON OF MAN *to* JOHN):   I turned to see the voice that was speaking to me, and saw seven golden lampstands. When I saw him, I fell at his feet as though dead. But he laid his right hand upon me.

SON OF MAN (*spotlight moves*):   Fear not, I am the first and the last, the living one; I died, and behold I am alive for evermore, and I have the keys of Death and Hades. Now write what you see, what is and what is to take place hereafter.

Scene 1

(SON OF MAN *lights the seven-branched menorah—slide for Ephesus in window*)

(Lights 1st candle— Candle of Greeting)

VOICE OFFSTAGE: To the angel of the church in Ephesus write:

(Lights 2nd candle— Candle of SON OF MAN)

The words of him who holds the seven stars in his right hand, who walks among the seven golden lampstands.

(Lights 3rd candle— Candle of Strength)

I know your work, your toil and your patient endurance. I know you are enduring patiently and bearing up for my name's sake, and you have not grown weary.

(Lights 4th candle— Candle of Weakness)

But I have this against you, that you have abandoned the love you had at first. . . .

(Lights 5th candle— Candle of Warning)	Repent and do the works you did at first. If not, I will come and remove your lampstand from its place.
(Lights 6th candle— Candle of Music)	CHOIR CHANTS: He who has an ear, let him hear what the Spirit says to the churches.
(Lights 7th candle— Candle of Reward)	To him who conquers I will grant to eat of the tree of life, which is in the paradise of God.

Scene 2

(SON OF MAN *lights the second menorah—slide of Smyrna appears in second window*)

(Lights 1st candle— Candle of Greeting)	VOICE OFFSTAGE: To the angel of the church in Smyrna write.
(Lights 2nd candle— Candle of SON OF MAN)	The words of the first and last, who died and came to life.
(Lights 3rd candle— Candle of Strength)	I know your tribulation and your poverty (but you are rich) and the slander of those who say that they are Jews and are not, but are a synagogue of Satan.
(Lights 4th candle— Candle of Weakness)	Silence! No weakness at Smyrna.
(Lights 5th candle— Candle of Warning)	Behold the devil is about to throw you into prison, that you may be tested, and for ten days you will have tribulation.
(Lights 6th candle— Candle of Music)	CHOIR CHANTS: He who has an ear, let him hear what the Spirit says to the churches. . . .
(Lights 7th candle— Candle of Reward)	I will give you the crown of life. He who conquers shall not be hurt by the second death.

Scene 3

(SON OF MAN *lights third menorah—slide of Pergamum appears in the third window*)

(Lights 1st candle— Candle of Greeting)	VOICE OFFSTAGE: To the angel of the church in Pergamum write:

(Lights 2nd candle—Candle of SON OF MAN)	The words of him who has the sharp two-edged sword.
(Lights 3rd candle—Candle of Strength)	I know where you dwell, where Satan's throne is; you hold fast my name and you did not deny my faith even in the days of Antipas my witness, my faithful one, who was killed among you, where Satan dwells.
(Lights 4th candle—Candle of Weakness)	But I have a few things against you: you have some there who hold the teaching of Balaam, who taught Balak to put a stumbling block before the sons of Israel, that they might eat food sacrificed to idols and practice immorality. So you also have some who hold the teaching of the Nicolaitans.
(Lights 5th candle—Candle of Warning)	Repent then. If not, I will come to you soon and war against them with the sword of my mouth.
(Lights 6th candle—Candle of Music)	CHOIR CHANTS: He who has an ear, let him hear what the Spirit says to the churches.
(Lights 7th candle—Candle of Reward)	To him who confesses I will give some of the hidden manna, and I will give him a white stone, with a new name written on the stone which no one knows except him who receives it.

Scene 4

(SON OF MAN *lights fourth menorah—slide of Thyatira appears in the fourth window*)

(Lights 1st candle—Candle of Greeting)	VOICE OFFSTAGE: To the angel of the church in Thyatira write:
(Lights 2nd candle—Candle of SON OF MAN)	The words of the Son of God, who has eyes like a flame of fire, and whose feet are like burnished bronze.
(Lights 3rd candle—Candle of Strength)	I know your words, your love and faith and service and patient endurance, and that your latter works exceed the first.
(Lights 4th candle—	But I have this against you, that you tolerate

Candle of Weakness)

the woman Jezebel, who calls herself a prophetess and is teaching my servants to practice immorality and to eat food sacrificed to idols.

(Lights 5th candle—
Candle of Warning)

I gave her time to repent, but she refuses to repent of her immorality. Behold, I will throw her on a sickbed, and those who commit adultery with her I will throw into great tribulation, unless they repent of her doings; and I will strike her children dead." . . .

(Lights 6th candle—
Candle of Reward)

He who conquers and who keeps my works until the end, I will give him power over the nations, and he shall rule them with a rod of iron, and I will give him the morning star.

(Lights 7th candle—
Candle of Music)

CHOIR CHANTS: He who has an ear, let him hear what the Spirit says to the churches.

Scene 5

(SON OF MAN *lights fifth menorah—slide of Sardis appears in the fifth window*)

(Lights 1st candle—
Candle of Greeting)

VOICE OFFSTAGE: To the angel of the church in Sardis write.

(Lights 2nd candle—
Candle of SON OF MAN)

The words of him who has the seven spirits of God and the seven stars.

(Lights 3rd candle—
Candle of Strength)

Silence! No strength in the church.

(Lights 4th candle—
Candle of Weakness)

I know your works; you have the name of being alive, and you are dead. I have not found your works perfect in the sight of my God.

(Lights 5th candle—
Candle of Warning)

Remember then what you received and heard; keep that and repent. If you will not awake I will come like a thief, and you will not know at what hour I will come upon you.

(Lights 6th candle—
Candle of Reward)

He who confesses shall be clothed thus in white garments, and I will not blot his name out of the book of life; I will confess his name before my father and before his angels.

(Lights 7th candle—   CHOIR CHANTS: He who has an ear, let him hear
Candle of Music)   what the Spirit says to the churches.

Scene 6

(SON OF MAN *lights sixth menorah—slide of Philadelphia appears in the
sixth window*)

(Lights 1st candle—   VOICE OFFSTAGE: To the angel of the church in
Candle of Greeting)   Philadelphia write:

(Lights 2nd candle—   The words of the holy one, the true one, who
Candle of SON OF MAN)   has the key of David, who opens and no one
                             shall shut, who shuts and no one opens.

(Lights 3rd candle—   I know your works. I know that you have but
Candle of Weakness)   little power, and yet you have kept my word
                             and have not denied my name.

(Lights 4th candle—   Silence! No weakness in the church.
Candle of Weakness)

(Lights 5th candle—   Hold fast what you have, so that no one may
Candle of Warning)   seize your crown.

(Lights 6th candle—   I will keep you from the hour of trial which is
Candle of Reward)   coming on the whole world. He who conquers
                             I will make him a pillar in the temple of my
                             God; never shall he go out of it, and I will write
                             on him the name of my God, and the name of
                             the city of my God.

(Lights 7th candle—   CHOIR CHANTS: He who has an ear, let him hear
Candle of Music)   what the Spirit says to the churches.

Scene 7

(SON OF MAN *lights seventh menorah—slide of Laodicea appears in the
seventh window*)

(Lights 1st candle—   VOICE OFFSTAGE: To the angel of the church in
Candle of Greeting)   Laodicea write:

(Lights 2nd candle—   The words of the Amen, the faithful and true
Candle of SON OF MAN)   witness, the beginning of God's creation.

(Lights 3rd candle— Candle of Strength)	Silence! No strength at Laodicea.
(Lights 4th candle— Candle of Weakness)	I know your works; you are neither cold or hot. For you say, I am rich, I have prospered, and I need nothing.
(Lights 5th candle— Candle of Warning)	Those whom I love, I reprove and chasten; so be zealous and repent.
(Lights 6th candle— Candle of Reward)	Behold, I stand at the door and knock; if any one hears my voice and opens the door, I will come in to him and eat with him, and he with me. He who conquers, I will grant to him to sit with me on my throne.
(Lights 7th candle— Candle of Music)	CHOIR CHANTS: He who has an ear, let him hear what the Spirit says to the churches.

(*At the end of the act, all seven windows of the stage building should be aglow with the seven lighted menorahs. JOHN and the SON OF MAN have their backs to the audience as they view the sight.*)

Act II
The Seven Seals
(Rev. 4:1 to 8:4)

STAGE SETTING: The heavenly court of God is located on the orchestra level of the stage. The altar of sacrifice (14 ft. tall) looms in the back of God's throne and immediately before the stage building.

(*Spotlight hits JOHN to right side of stage.*)

JOHN: I looked, and lo, in heaven an open door. And the first voice, which I had heard speaking to me like a trumpet.

VOICE: Come up hither and I will show you what must happen after this.

JOHN: At once I was in the Spirit, and lo, a throne stood in heaven.

(*Back floor spotlight behind throne comes on.*)

JOHN: Seated on the throne was one who appeared like jasper and carnelian.

(*Front overhead spotlights center of throne.*)

JOHN: Round the throne was a rainbow; its emerald color represented eternal life. God's complete revelation, old and new covenants, was represented by twenty-four elders seated on thrones around God's throne.

(*Dim overhead spotlight lights up entire throne area.*)

JOHN: These elders represented the twelve tribes of Israel and Jesus' twelve disciples. Their white dress symbolized their spiritual bodies. Before the throne were seven burning torches which stand for the Holy Spirit, and around the throne was what looked like a sea of glass. It was clear as crystal.

(*Overhead spotlight brightens, lighting entire throne area.*)

JOHN: In the center around the throne were four living creatures who symbolized all of God's created order. Each was covered with eyes showing their divine presence and each had six wings indicating their imperfection.

(*Four actors dressed in black come forward as they are introduced carrying silk banners with faces of lion, ox, man, and eagle.*)

JOHN: The first was like a lion representing all wild creatures. The second was like an ox representing all domestic creatures. The third was like a man representing intelligent life. The fourth an eagle represented all flying creatures. Day and night they never stopped praising him who sat upon the throne.

CHOIR: Holy, holy, holy, is the Lord God Almighty, who was and is and is to come!

JOHN: The elders joined in worshiping him who lives forever.

(*Elders fall down in front of throne and bow in worship.*)

CHOIR: Worthy art thou, our Lord and God, to receive glory and honor and power, for thou didst create all things, and by thy will they existed and were created.

(*Elders return to thrones at end of second hymn.*)

JOHN: I saw in the right hand of him who was seated on the throne a scroll written within and on the back. It was sealed seven times, indicating that it was a divine book. And I saw a strong angel proclaiming with a loud voice.

STRONG ANGEL: Who is worthy to open the scroll and break its seals?

JOHN: And no one in heaven or on earth or under the earth, was able to open the scroll or to look into it. I wept much that no one was found worthy to open the scroll.

ELDER: Weep not, lo, the Lion of Judah, the Root of David, has conquered, so that he can open the scroll and its seven seals.

(*An actor dressed in black carrying a banner bearing the image of a lamb enters the chorus level.*)

JOHN: I saw a Lamb standing, as though it had been slain. He had seven horns a sign of his divine strength and power and seven eyes which represent his divine insight. And he went and took the scroll from the right hand of him who was seated upon the throne. When he had done this, the elders and the creatures fell down before him singing a hymn of praise!

CHOIR: Worthy art thou to take the scroll and to open its seals, for thou wast slain and by thy blood didst ransom men for God from every tribe and tongue and people and nation, and hast made them a kingdom and priests to our God, and they shall reign on earth.

JOHN: Then thousands of angels joined in the singing before God's throne.

CHOIR: Worthy is the Lamb who was slain, to receive power and wealth and wisdom and might and honor and glory and blessing!

JOHN: Then I heard every creature in heaven and on earth and under the earth and in the sea join in the praise.

CHOIR (*to be sung very loudly*): To him who sits upon the throne and to the Lamb be blessing and honor and glory and might for ever and ever!

FOUR CREATURES: Amen!

(*Dim lights. Elders and creatures move back to central stage.*)

Scenes 1—4

JOHN: And I saw the Lamb open the first seal, and heard the first living creature call:

LION CREATURE: Come!

(*Strike gong or cymbal.*)

(*Show slide of white horse.*)

JOHN: Behold! A white horse came forth, symbolizing conquest. The rider held a bow and a crown was given to him and he rode away to conquer.

JOHN: I saw the Lamb break the second seal and the second living creature spoke:

OX CREATURE: Come!

(*Strike gong or cymbal.*)

(*Show slide of red horse.*)

JOHN: Then came a red horse, symbolizing war and destruction. The rider was given power to take peace from the world, and received a large sword.

JOHN: The Lamb broke open the third seal and the third living creature called out:

MAN CREATURE: Come!

(*Strike gong or cymbal.*)

(*Show slide of black horse.*)

JOHN: Behold a black horse! Its rider held a pair of scales. The black horse brings famine—the scales represent the measure of a day's ration of food.

JOHN: I saw the Lamb open the fourth seal and the fourth living creature spoke!

EAGLE CREATURE: Come!

(*Strike gong or cymbal.*)

(*Show slide of pale green horse.*)

JOHN: Behold I saw a pale green horse, and its rider was Death and close behind the horse came Hades! They were given power to kill one fourth of all the earth, to kill with the sword, with famine, with pestilence, and wild beasts.

(*Lights are turned out—a group of people move to altar of sacrifice and fall at its base.*)

Scene 5

(*Spotlight altar area.*)

JOHN: I saw the Lamb open the fifth seal!

(*Strike gong or cymbal.*)

(*Slide of people in white robes in window 5.*)

JOHN: I beheld under the altar the souls of those who were martyred for their faith in the Lamb.

MARTYRS (*in unison*): Oh Sovereign Lord, holy and true, how long, before thou wilt judge and avenge our blood on those who dwell upon the earth?

LAMB: You must rest a little longer, until the number of your fellow servants and brethren should be complete, those who are yet to be martyred for their faith.

JOHN: The Lamb gave them each a white robe, a symbol of resurrection bodies.

(*Those by the altar should be given white robes.*)

Scene 6

VOICE: And he opened the sixth seal!

(*Strike gong or cymbal.*)

(*All lights go out except spotlight on* JOHN. *Show slide of black sun and moon like blood.*)

JOHN (*starting off quietly and building to a loud conclusion*): As I saw the sixth seal broken there was a great earthquake, a sign of the overthrow of the world's political order and the judgment of the ungodly. The sun became black as sackcloth. The full month became like blood, the stars fell to the earth, and the sky vanished like a scroll. Every mountain and island was removed from its place. The kings, the great men, the commanders, the rich, the strong, every slave and free man hid in the caves and among the rocks of the mountains and calling out:

CHOIR (*chants*): Fall on us and hide us from the presence of him who sits on the throne, and from the wrath of the Lamb; for the great day of judgment has come, and who can stand before it?

(*As* JOHN *finishes speaking, lights flash on and off then there is a loud clap of thunder and all lights go out.*)

Interlude

(*After a brief period of silence, the spotlight falls on* JOHN *and as he speaks there is a sound of wind and the slide of the four angels holding back the winds appears on the screen.*)

JOHN: After this I saw four angels standing at the four corners of the earth, holding back the four winds of the wrath of God.

ANGEL: Do not harm the earth or sea or the trees, till we have sealed the servants of our God upon their foreheads.

JOHN: 144,000 people were sealed—all true believers. 144,000 represents completeness.

(*Spotlight focuses on Christians just below* JOHN *at right of stage as angel comes forth and seals Christians.*)

CHOIR (*chants*):   Salvation belongs to our God who sits upon the throne and to the Lamb!

JOHN: When these people had made this cry, the angels, the elders, and the four beasts all fell on their faces and worshiped God.

CHOIR: Amen! blessing, glory, wisdom and thanksgiving, and honor, and power, and might be unto our God forever.

JOHN: Then one of the elders told me who this great number of people was.

ELDER: They are all dressed in white because they have overcome; they have endured to the end, and have washed their robes in the blood of the Lamb. They have come out of the great tribulation.

CHOIR: Therefore are they before the throne of God, and serve him day and night within his temple; and he who sits upon the throne will shelter them with his presence. They shall hunger no more, neither thirst any more; the sun shall not strike them, nor any scorching heat. For the Lamb in the midst of the throne will be their shepherd, and he will guide them to springs of living water; and God will wipe away every tear from their eyes.

Scene 7

(*All lights go out—* ELDERS *move back to thrones.*)

(*The altar of incense should replace the altar of sacrifice and the seven angels for the next act should form on the stage.*)

VOICE: And he opened the seventh seal!

(*Strike gong or cymbal.*)

(*Spotlight on* JOHN—*throne area lighted dimly.*)

JOHN: The Lamb broke open the seventh seal, there was complete silence in heaven for about one half hour.

(*Silence for about two minutes.*)

JOHN: Then I saw the seven angels who stand before God. They were given seven trumpets. Another angel, who had a golden incense container, came and stood at the altar. He was given much incense to mingle with the prayers of all of God's people. As I saw the smoke from the burning incense go up with the prayers of God's people I understood that there is hope for those being persecuted and that God does hear the prayers of his people. They will receive mercy and protection from the coming judgment. Then the angel took the incense container and filled it with fire from the altar and threw it upon the earth. All around there was rumbling, peals of thunder, flashes of lightning, and an earthquake greatly shook the earth.

(*Sound and light effects again create thunder and lightning.*)

JOHN: In Act II, I saw the four great forces that will sweep across the stage of the world, over and over again: conquering war, famine, and death. In the midst of that Christians will be persecuted. Yet there was also a message of hope for believers. God will one day judge the world, true believers will be sealed and will not receive God's judgments and their prayers will be heard, even in the midst of their persecution.

Act III
The Seven Trumpets
(Rev. 8:5 to 11:18)

Characters: JOHN, EAGLE, VOICE, ANGEL, 7 ANGELS with long silver trumpets.

STAGE SETTING: The altar of sacrifice is replaced with the altar of incense on the chorus area. JOHN remains on the *proskene*. God's throne room with chorus and living creatures remains in chorus level.

JOHN: Then the seven angels with the seven trumpets prepared to blow them.
(*Seven members of chorus move up onto the ledge with trumpets in hand, and stand in front of each of the seven windows, with trumpets in an "at the ready" position—such as in "present arms."*)

Scene 1

JOHN: The first angel blew his trumpet. (ANGEL *steps forward to the edge of the ledge and plays.*)

(*Slide in the first window depicts the scene, as narrated.*)

Hail and fire, mixed with blood, fell on the earth. A third of the earth was burnt up, a third of the trees, and every blade of grass.

Scene 2

JOHN: Then the second angel blew his trumpet. (ANGEL *steps forward to the edge of the ledge and plays.*)

Something like a great mountain burning with fire was thrown into the sea. A third of the sea became blood, a third of the living creatures in the sea died, and a third of the ships were destroyed.

Scene 3

JOHN: Then the third angel blew his trumpet. (ANGEL *steps forward, plays.*)

A large star fell from heaven, burning like a torch, and upon a third of the rivers and on the springs of water. A third of the water became bitter, and many people died from drinking the water, because it was made bitter.

Scene 4

JOHN: Then the fourth angel blew his trumpet. (ANGEL *steps forward, plays.*)

A third of the sun was struck, and a third of the moon, and a third of the stars, so that their light lost a third of its brightness; a third of the day was kept from shining, and likewise a third of the night.

JOHN: Then I looked, and I heard an eagle that was flying high in the air cry in a loud voice,

EAGLE (*member of choir with eagle mask*):   Woe, woe, woe to those who dwell on earth when the sound comes from the trumpets that the other three angels must blow.

Scene 5

JOHN: Then the fifth angel blew his trumpet. (ANGEL *steps forward, plays.*)

JOHN: I saw a star fallen from heaven to earth and he was given the key of the shaft of the bottomless pit. He opened up this pit and smoke rose up like the smoke of a giant furnace. Then from the smoke came locusts on the earth.

(*Choir members with locust masks walk across the ledge.*)

They were told not to harm the grass of the earth or any tree but only those people who have not the seal of God upon their foreheads. They were like horses arrayed for battle; on their heads were crowns of gold; their faces were like human faces; their hair like women's hair; their teeth like lion's teeth. They had scales like iron breastplates, and the noise of their wings was like the noise of many chariots with horses rushing into battle; they had tails like scorpions, and stings. They went about the earth torturing people for five months. Their king is Abaddon.

(*The first woe is over; after this there are still two more woes to come.*)

Scene 6

Then the sixth angel blew his trumpet. (ANGEL *steps forward, plays.*)

JOHN: I heard a voice coming from the four corners of the gold altar standing before God. The voice said to the sixth angel,

VOICE (*offstage*): Release the four angels who are bound at the great river Euphrates.

JOHN: The four angels were released; for this very hour of this very day of this very month and year they had been kept ready to kill a third of all mankind.

JOHN: I was told the number of the mounted troops: it was two hundred million. And in my vision I saw the horses and their riders: they had breastplates red as fire, blue as sapphire, and yellow as sulphur. The horses' heads were like lions' heads, and from their mouths came out fire, smoke, and sulphur. A third of mankind was killed by those three plagues: the fire, the smoke, and the sulphur. For the power of the horses was in their mouths and also in their tails. Their tails were like snakes with heads, and by means of them they wounded people.

The rest of mankind, all those who had not been killed by these plagues, did not turn away from what they themselves had made. They did not stop worshiping demons, nor the idols of gold, silver, bronze, stone, and wood, which cannot see, hear, or walk. Nor did they repent of their murders, their magic, their immorality, or their stealing.

Then I saw another mighty angel coming down out of heaven. He was wrapped in a cloud and had a rainbow around his head; his face was like the sun, and his legs were like columns of fire. He had a small scroll open in his hand. He put his right foot on the sea and his left foot on the land, and called out in a loud voice that sounded like the roar of lions.

ANGEL (*standing on ramp nearest narrator*):   (*He gives a loud cry.*)

JOHN: After he had called out, the seven thunders answered with a roar. (*timpani roll offstage*) As soon as they spoke, I was about to write, but I heard a voice speak from heaven.

VOICE (*offstage*):   Seal up what the seven thunders have said; do not write it down.

JOHN: Then the angel that I saw standing on the sea and on the land raised his right hand to heaven and took a vow in the name of God, who lives forever and ever, who created heaven, earth, and the sea, and everything in them. The angel said,

ANGEL: Let there be no more delay. But when the seventh angel blows his trumpet, then God will accomplish his secret plan, as he announced to his servants, the prophets.

JOHN: Then the voice that I had heard speaking from heaven spoke to me again, saying,

VOICE: Go and take the open scroll which is in the hand of the angel standing on the sea and on the land.

JOHN (*moving toward the angel on the ramp*):   I went to the angel and asked him to give me the little scroll. He said to me,

ANGEL: Take it and eat; it will be bitter to your stomach, but sweet as honey in your mouth.

(JOHN *picks up the scroll and reads it closely.*)

JOHN: I took the little scroll from his hand and ate it, and it tasted sweet as honey in my mouth. But after I swallowed it, it became bitter in my stomach.

ANGEL: Once again you must proclaim God's message about many nations, races, languages and kings. (Moves across ledge toward John.)

JOHN: I was then given a stick (*by angel*) that looked like a measuring rod.

ANGEL: Rise and measure the temple of God and the altar, and count those who are worshiping there. But do not measure the outer courts, because they have been given to the Gentiles, who will trample on the Holy City for forty-two months. I will send my two witnesses dressed in sackcloth and they will proclaim God's message during those 1,260 days.

JOHN: The two witnesses are the two olive trees and the two lamps that stand before the Lord of the earth. If anyone tries to harm them, fire comes out of their mouths and destroys their enemies; and in this way whoever tries to harm them will be killed. They have authority to shut up the sky so that there will be no rain during the time they proclaim God's message. They have authority also over the springs of water, to turn them into blood; they have authority also to strike the earth with every kind of plague as often as they wish.

When they finish proclaiming their message, the beast that comes up out of the bottomless pit will fight against them. He will defeat them and kill them, and their bodies will lie in the street of the great city, where their Lord was crucified. The symbolic name of that city is Sodom, or Egypt. People from all nations, tribes, languages, and races will look at their bodies for three and a half days and will not allow them to be buried. The people of the earth will be happy because of the death of these two. They will celebrate and send presents to each other, because those two prophets brought much suffering upon mankind.

After three and a half days a life-giving breath came from God and entered them, and they stood up; and all who saw them were terrified. Then the two prophets heard a loud voice say to them from heaven, "Come up here." As their enemies watched, they went up into heaven in a cloud. At that very moment there was a violent earthquake; a tenth of the city was destroyed, and seven thousand people were killed. The rest of the people were terrified and praised the greatness of the God of heaven.

The second woe is over, but the third woe will come soon.

Then the seventh angel blew his trumpet. (*Angel steps forward, plays.*)

There were loud voices in heaven, saying,

VOICES (*several members of chorus*): The power to rule over the world belongs now to our Lord and his Messiah, and he will rule forever and ever.

JOHN: Then the twenty-four elders who sit on their thrones in front of God threw themselves face downward and worshiped God, saying,

CHORUS: We give thanks to thee, Lord God Almighty, who art and who wast, that thou has taken thy great power and begun to reign. The nations raged, but thy wrath came, and the time for the dead to be judged, for rewarding thy servants, the prophets and saints, and those who fear thy name, both small and great, and for destroying the destroyers of the earth.

JOHN: In Act III, I saw God's incomplete judgment—one third of things destroyed. If you have eyes of faith, you can see God's hand of judgment at work in the world. Yet there was a message of hope for believers: they have been measured or protected, and God's living Word—the two witnesses—cannot be destroyed.

Act IV
The Seven Tableaux
(Rev. 11:19 to 15:4)

Characters: JOHN, BANNER CARRIERS, CHOIR, BEAST, ANGELS.

STAGE SETTING: The orchestra level will remain as in previous acts with the exception of the ark of the covenant replacing the altars of Acts II and III. The chorus is at front stage, surrounding the throne.

The focal point of the temple in Act IV is the holy of holies behind the throne of God at center stage. As the act begins, the holy of holies is shown open with a spotlight on the ark only. The rest of the stage is dark with floodlights coming up slowly to brighten the stage.

The Choir which ended Act III with a song of thanksgiving should still be singing with their voices fading until unintelligible. Lights flicker to indicate lightning and the gong sounds to represent thunder, as the fourth act begins.

(*A revolving door, called an* eccyclema *should be placed in window 1 to provide three subscenes.*)

Scene 1

Stage Directions: *Full lights slowly dimming to a gold spot on the ark and a white spot on the woman. A member of the chorus, a woman, enters from left and walks to left center. She is clothed in white and gold and is wearing a crown of twelve stars. The woman is obviously pregnant and in the pains of imminent birth. She is crying out in her pain.*

As John begins to speak, the picture of woman and child appears in the first window of the skene.

JOHN (*right center stage,* proskene *level*):   And a great sign appeared in heaven a woman clothed with the sun, with the moon under her feet, and on her head a crown of twelve stars; and she was with child; and she cried out in her pangs of birth in anguish for delivery.

(*First picture off.*)

(*As* JOHN *finishes speaking, another member of the chorus dressed in black approaches the woman from right stage. He is carrying a banner depicting the red dragon with seven heads. As the member moves, a red spotlight follows him.*)

JOHN: And another sign appeared in heaven; behold, a great red dragon with seven heads and ten horns, and seven diadems upon his heads. His tail swept down a third of the stars of heaven, and cast them to the earth. And the dragon stood before the woman who was about to bear a child that he might devour her child. And the dragon's name was Satan.

(*As John speaks, the dragon threatens the woman and stands before her facing her. He stretches out his arms to hide her as if overwhelming her. The woman screams. Lights flash as the woman runs from the dragon to the left. She hesitates and then escapes. [Dramatic music or effect. Satan remains.]*)

As John speaks, with great victorious music in the background, the woman enters from stage left carrying a baby. She goes to the ark and presents the child to the audience. Then she goes to the right, is threatened by the dragon, and exits on the left of stage to an area depicting the wilderness. Eccyclema is turned to show second scene of the child's rescue.)

JOHN: And she brought forth a male child, one who is to rule all the nations with a rod of iron; but her child was caught up to God and to his throne, and the woman fled into the wilderness where she has a place prepared by God, in which to be nourished for one thousand two hundred and sixty days.

(Eccyclema *is turned to show third scene of war in heaven.*)

(*Lights are turned up full. Satan has remained on stage right and is joined by three black-robed angels at the right. They advance toward the woman in the wilderness and are met by Michael and two angels. A battle ensues. Satan is cast [pushed] to the right stage where he cowers. The black angels are beaten down and begin to crawl off the stage [right]. As John speaks, Michael and his companions exit.*)

JOHN (*accompanied by triumphant music*):   Now war arose in heaven, Michael and his angels fighting against the dragon. And the dragon and his angels fought, but they were defeated, and there was no longer any place for them in heaven. And the great dragon was thrown down to the earth, and his angels were thrown down with him. And I heard a loud voice in heaven, saying:

CHOIR (*slowly, but triumphantly*):   Now the salvation, and the power, and the kingdom of our God and the authority of his Christ have come, for the accuser of our brethren has been thrown down, who accuses them day and night before our God. And they have conquered him by the blood of the Lamb and because of the word of their testimony, for they loved not their lives even unto death. Rejoice, O heaven and you who dwell therein! Woe to you, O earth and sea, for the devil has come down to you in great wrath, because he knows that his time is short!

(*Lights dim with one spotlight on the woman in the wilderness to the left side of the stage. The woman is being nourished in the wilderness. Another light shines on Satan who is standing on the right side of the stage. He looks around, sees the woman, and moves toward her. As Satan approaches the woman, two white angels surround and protect the woman and fend off Satan as they escort her to safety to the left and exit. Satan follows behind as John speaks.*)

JOHN: And when the dragon saw that he had been thrown down to the earth, he pursued the woman who had given birth to the male child. And the two wings of the great eagle were given to the woman, in order that she might fly into the wilderness to her place, where she is to be nourished for a time and times and half a time. The serpent poured water like a river out of his mouth after the woman, to sweep her away with the flood. And the earth helped the woman, and the earth opened its mouth and swallowed the river which the dragon poured out of his mouth.

(*After the woman and good angels have exited off at stage left, the spotlight with red tint focuses on Satan at left of stage. Satan is angry and comes back across the stage taunting the audience, and making gestures. Then as the scene closes, Satan is standing on stage left and looking out across the moat [sea of glass], and as lights begin to dim, John speaks.*)

JOHN: Then the dragon was angry with the woman, and went off to make war with the rest of her offspring, who keep the commandments of God and bear testimony to Jesus.

(*Lights dim. White spotlight is on John and second window. The gold spotlight remains on the ark in the holy of holies.*)

Scene 2

(*In the second window appears the depiction of the beast of the sea. A person wearing black carries a banner with the beast painted on it. The beast enters from the lower stage area by the moat, left. The choir moans and shrieks. Strobe lights flash dimly as the beast approaches.*)

(*As John begins to read, the spotlight follows the beast who slowly moves around the stage. All but two individuals are bowing down to the beast. These two represent saints who are trying to flee from his authority.*)

JOHN: And I saw a beast rising out of the sea. He had ten horns and seven heads, with ten crowns on his horns. On each head was the blasphemous name of a different emperor. The beast was like a leopard, as Babylon; had feet like that of Media, the bear, and a mouth like the lion of Rome. The dragon gave the beast his power. The whole world was astonished and followed the beast. Men worshiped the dragon because he had given political authority to the beast. The beast was given a mouth to utter proud words and blasphemies and to exercise his authority for forty-two months. He opened his mouth to blaspheme God and to slander his name and his dwelling place and those in heaven. This beast represents the political power of Rome.

BEAST: Bow and worship me. I have all power; God is nothing. God is dead.

PEOPLE (*those bowing*): Who is like the beast, and who can fight against him?

(*During this, the other two also bow down and begin worshiping him.*)

JOHN: He was given power to make war against the saints and to conquer them and authority over every tribe, people, language, and nation. All inhabitants of the earth will worship the beast whose names have not been written in the book of life belonging to the Lamb that was slain from the foundation of the world.

CHOIR: He who has an ear, let him hear. If anyone is to go into captivity, he will go. If anyone is to be killed with the sword, with the sword he will be killed.

JOHN: Here is a call for the endurance and faith of the saints.

(*Lights dim.*)

Scene 3

(*The third window showing the beast of the land appears. A person wear-*

ing black carries a banner with a painting of the beast from the land on it. Evil, howling music is heard in the background. The stage is set just as it was at the end of Scene 2 and a spotlight focuses in on John who is holding a scroll.)

JOHN: Then I saw another beast, which rose out of the earth. It had two horns like a lamb and spoke like a dragon. It had all the power of the first beast and caused all of the earth to worship this first beast, whose deadly wound was healed. It represented the worship of political power.

(As John speaks, the second beast who is lying on the floor in a long black robe arises slowly and begins to move about the stage making gestures to the audience. He then leads several of the chorus members in worshiping the first beast.)

JOHN: The beast of the land performed great miracles, even calling fire to come down from heaven onto the earth in the sight of all men.

(Fire is shown as a flashing of lights and possibly streamers from the beast.)

JOHN: And through these miracles it deceived all of the earth. It ordered them to set up a statue of the first beast and even gave life to that statue so that it would speak.

(The second beast goes over to the first beast which has been standing idly and causes it to move and scream a great scream so that all of the chorus is terrified.)

JOHN: It ordered that everyone was to worship this first beast. And all who worshiped him were given a mark that they might buy and sell, and without the mark a man could buy nothing.

(The second beast moves over to the chorus members and places a mark on their hands, a tattoo of Caesar's face. When they have received this mark, they bow down to the first beast and exit the stage. As they exit a deep voice is heard in the background stating, "Here is wisdom. Let him that has understanding count the number of the beast for it is the number of a man; and his number is . . ." Many voices join in to chant—"666").

(Lights dim and spotlight focuses on fourth window.)

Scene 4

(The fourth window opens, portraying the Lamb standing on Mount Zion and with him is the 144,000. They have the Lamb's name and his father's

name written on their foreheads in clear view. As the door opens, a bright white spotlight focuses on a choir member elevated slightly above the other choir members. This choir member, displaying the Lamb banner, represents the true Lamb and stands in center stage close to the throne. Six other choir members dressed in white stand directly behind the one who represents the true Lamb.

The scene opens with a rush of water that is consistent in sound and rhythm. A loud drum roll begins with a cymbal clash and, as it is repeated, becomes softer and less rhythmical to portray the sound of loud thunder. John stands right center on the proskene.)

JOHN: Then I looked, and behold, the Lamb stood on Mount Zion, and the 144,000 who had his and his father's name stood with him. And I heard a voice from heaven like the rush of many waters and the roar of loud thunder; the voice was like the sound of harpists playing their harps.

(The six choir members will slowly and softly begin strumming their harps and hum excitedly, depicting that their song is a new song and they are the only ones who can sing it.)

JOHN: And they sing a new song before the throne and before the four living creatures and before the elders. No one could learn that song except the hundred and forty-four thousand who had been redeemed. These have not defiled themselves with women, for they are chaste, they follow the Lamb wherever he goes, they have been redeemed from mankind as firstfruits for God and the Lamb, and in their mouth no lie was found, for they are sinless.

(The six choir members follow after the Lamb on center stage who parades with authority. As the choir members follow the Lamb, they appear reverent and keep their eyes on him at all times.

The scene ends with the Lamb leading the processional offstage left and out of view of the audience.)

Interlude

(Angels in white robes enter the proskene *from stage left. The stage is darkened except for the illuminated paintings in the* thuromata. *A white spot follows each angel to center stage where their respective announcements are made to the audience in a voice of firm authority. The first angel enters as John speaks.)*

JOHN: I saw another angel flying between heaven and earth. He proclaimed an eternal gospel to all who inhabit earth; to those of every nation, language and custom. His clear voice was audible to all.

FIRST ANGEL (*speaking in a resonant voice to earth below*):   Fear God alone and give him glory because the decisive hour of his judgment has come. Worship the one who made the heavens and earth and all that is in them.

(FIRST ANGEL *exits stage right. Spot follows* first angel *off, then follows* SECOND ANGEL *on. As* JOHN *begins to speak,* SECOND ANGEL *enters from stage right.*)

JOHN: Then there was a second angel who followed the first. He sounded forth a pronouncement of destruction as a proclamation of salvation.

SECOND ANGEL (*speaking as with a shout of victory*):   Fallen, fallen is Babylon the great who seduced the nations to intoxicate themselves by her impure passion for power.

(SECOND ANGEL *exits stage right followed by white spotlight. Immediately another white spot moves to* THIRD ANGEL *at stage left. He walks boldly to center stage and stops.*)

THIRD ANGEL (*in a bold, deep, threatening voice*):   If anyone worships the beast and his image and receives the mark on the forehead or hand he will fall under the fury of God's wrath. He will be tormented with burning sulfur in the presence of the holy angels and of the Lamb—forever.

CHORUS: This is a call for endurance on the part of the saints who obey God's commandments and remain faithful to Jesus.

(*Immediately a loud, monotonic voice offstage proclaims the following and John looks up, startled, and searches for the source.*)

LOUD VOICE: Blessed are the dead who die in the Lord from now on.

(*Lights dim.*)

Scene 5

(*Spotlight focuses on the fifth window where there is a picture of the Son of Man on a white cloud. The spotlight shifts to the Son of Man as he enters from stage left. On his head is a golden crown, and there is a sickle in his hand. An angel comes out of the Temple and speaks to the Son of Man.*)

ANGEL: Take your sickle and reap, for the time to reap has come and the harvest of the earth is ripe.

(*White spotlights are on the angel and the* SON OF MAN. *The* SON OF MAN *then stands and begins swinging his sickle in the act of harvesting. Then there is a drum roll along with several cymbal clangs. Lights dim.*)

Scene 6

(*In the sixth window of the* proskene *appears the image of an angel harvesting grapes and the image of a winepress from which flows blood up to the height of a horse's bridle. Prior to the lights coming up, several bunches of artificial grapes have been placed on the stage.*

From stage left an angel comes out of the Temple carrying a sharp sickle. In his other hand he has a depiction of fire (a flaming lighter). *A second angel enters and walks to the other one. They stand together, center front.*)

ANGEL 2:   Stretch out your sickle, and gather the earth's grape harvest, for its clusters are ripe.

(*The* FIRST ANGEL *approaches the front of the stage with a sickle. A banner should cross the stage showing clusters of grapes and then another one showing a winepress. Stage is flooded with red light as the cymbal clangs and the first angel swings the sickle.*)

JOHN: The angel put his sickle to the earth and gathered in its grapes, and threw them into the great winepress of God's wrath. The winepress of God was trodden outside the city, and for sixteen hundred stadia, which is interpreted 200 miles, blood flowed from the press to the height of the horses' bridles.

(ANGEL *stomps on the grapes and the stage is flooded in red light. Then lights dim and angels exit stage.*)

Scene 7

(*Spotlight focuses on the seventh window, where there are shown seven angels pouring out seven plagues of Act V. They pour their bowls into the sea, turning it red to reveal God's wrath. Beside the sea of glass, on the orchestra level, are chorus members with harps. These are the ones who had victory over the beast. They are singing.*)

JOHN: Then I saw another sign in heaven. There were seven angels with seven plagues which are the last of God's wrath to be revealed. I also saw a sea of glass mingled with fire and those that had victory over the beast stood by the sea of glass with harps in their hands singing the song of the Lamb.

CHORUS 1:   Great and wonderful are thy deeds,

CHORUS 2:   O Lord God Almighty!

CHORUS 1:   Just and true are thy ways,

CHORUS 2:   Thou art the King of the ages!

ALL: Who shall not be in fear and glorify thy name, O Lord?

CHORUS 1:   For thou alone art holy.

CHORUS 2:   All nations shall come and worship thee.

(*Short pause*)

ALL: For thy judgments have been revealed.

(*Lights dim.*)

JOHN: In Act IV, I saw the struggle between good and evil down through world history. This battle began with Satan's attempts to destroy the Messiah. Satan was cast down to earth where he sought to use political power to control the earth. In the ancient world, he used the Caesars. However, in every age he uses other political power. He turns such power into a religious worship service like Caesar worship. However, against him stands the Lamb and his followers—they will be triumphant.

Act V
The Seven Bowls of Wrath
(Rev. 15:5 to 16:21)

Characters: JOHN, CHOIR, CHORAL READING GROUPS, SON OF MAN

STAGE SETTING: The stage will be in the same setting as Act IV except the ark of the covenant will not be seen. A long bench will be placed beside the screen with seven bowls containing a mixture of confetti and glitter. Two angels will be standing offstage clothed in white robes with golden sashes. John will be standing upstage left. CHORUS will be facing stage with their backs to the audience. Smoke comes forth from the holy of holies and the sea of glass turns red as blood. Change blue light around the choir level to red.

Prologue

(*Stage dark—spotlight on* JOHN'S *face—timpani roll begins 'pp' and crescendo throughout*)

JOHN: Then I looked, and the Temple, of the tent of witness, that is in heaven was opened. Out of the Temple came the seven angels with the seven plagues. They were robed in pure, bright linen and wore golden sashes around their chests. (*Chimes begin.*) Then one of the four living creatures gave to the seven angels seven golden bowls (*white spotlight appears on bowls and follows bowls throughout the sequence of the whole act. Spot beam is to be at its smallest while bowls are on bench and gradually enlarge while angel pours out bowl and then spot shrinks to original size until next angel picks up the next bowl*) filled with the wrath of God, who lives forever and ever. (*Cymbal roll begins.*) And the Temple was filled with smoke from the glory of God and from his power, and no one could enter the Temple until the seven plagues of the seven angels were ended.

(*Instruments cut off at the word* ended—*brief silence, then:*)

JOHN: Then I heard a loud voice from the Temple telling the seven angels,

CHOIR (*dim white floor light on chorus*):   Go, pour out the seven bowls of God's wrath on the earth. (*Spotlight on* JOHN *dims to half strength.*)

Scene 1

(*Timpani cadence—first angel steps forward and pours out bowl as* READER 1 [JOHN] *begins. Dim white floor light changes to dim green floor light on chorus and remains throughout scene.*)

JOHN: The first angel went and poured out his bowl on the earth . . . (*Pause until action of angel is near completion. Slide of plague appears in window 1.*)

JOHN (*slide 1*): and foul and evil sores broke out . . .

CHOIR: . . . on all the people. (*Chorus immediately softens to just above a whisper and repeats "all the people" till the word* image *in the next phrase.*)

JOHN (JOHN *allows choir to chant the phrase 3 times, then joins them and continues his part*):

. . . all the people who bore the mark of the beast and worshiped its image.

CHOIR: Yea, Lord God the Almighty, true and just are thy judgments!

(*Stage darkens—pause.*)

Scene 2

(*Timpani cadence—second angel steps forward and pours out bowl as* JOHN *begins to read. Dim blue floor light on chorus.*)

JOHN: The second angel poured out his bowl into the sea, ... (*Pause until action is near completion.*)

JOHN: (*As second reading begins, blue light changes to dim red and slide 2 comes on*) and it became the blood of a dead man, ...

CHOIR (*pause*):   and every living thing in the sea ... (*cut all lights and slide before final chorus word*) died.

(*Pause—dim white lights on chorus before final line.*)

CHOIR: Yea, Lord God the Almighty, true and just are thy judgments!

(*Pause*)

Scene 3

(*Timpani cadence—third angel steps forward and pours out bowl as reader begins.*)

JOHN (*change dim white floor light to dim blue floor light during* READER 1):   Then the third angel poured his bowl into the rivers and fountains of the earth.

JOHN (*dim blue floor lights mixed with red floor lights as slide 3 is shown*):   And they became blood (*dim blue light completely fades, leaving only dim red floor lights; spot on* JOHN *increases to full intensity*).

JOHN: And I heard the angel of the water say,

SOLO SINGER: Just art thou in these thy judgments,
Thou who art and wast, O Holy One.
For men have shed the blood of saints and prophets,
And thou hast given them blood to drink,
It is their due!

JOHN: And I heard the altar cry,

(*Stage lights dim—go to white spot on chorus.*)

CHOIR: Yea, Lord God the Almighty, true and just are thy judgments!

(*All lights dim—pause.*)

Scene 4

(*Timpani cadence—fourth angel steps forward and pours out bowl as John begins to read.*)

JOHN (*dim yellow floor lights*):   The fourth angel poured his bowl on the sun.

(*As angel pours bowl, mix red and yellow floor lights to give fiery orange effect, slide 4.*)

CHORAL GROUP I (*chanting*):   And all were scorched by fire,

CHORAL GROUP II (*chanting*):   And with fierce heat.

GROUP I: And they cursed the name of God,

CHOIR: And they did not repent! (*Crescendo*)

(*Brief moment of silence and dim all lights; then strong spot on chorus.*)

CHOIR: Yea, Lord God the Almighty, true and just are thy judgments. (*Kill lights—pause.*)

Scene 5

(*Timpani cadence—dim blue floor lights. Fifth angel steps forward and pours out bowl as John begins to read.*)

JOHN: And the fifth angel poured his bowl upon the throne of the beast. (*All lights dim as slide 5—a picture of ancient Rome or Roman ruins is shown.*)

GROUP I: And its kingdom was in darkness.

GROUP II: They gnawed their tongues in anguish. (*Moaning in background —low timpani roll*)

GROUP I: And they cursed the God of heaven. . . .

CHOIR: And they did not repent! (*Crescendo.*)

(*Pause—then white spot, spread on chorus.*)

CHOIR: Yea, Lord God the Almighty, true and just are thy judgments!

Scene 6

(*Timpani rolls into a crescendo. At top of crescendo, spot hits John. Chorus is in the dark. Sixth angel steps forward and pours out bowl as John begins to read.*)

JOHN: The sixth angel poured his bowl on the great river Euphrates

(*As reader speaks, slowly bring up blue lights on* CHORUS.)

CHOIR (*Slide 6—Euphrates River*): and its water was dried up, to prepare the way for the kings from the east.

JOHN: And I saw issuing from the mouth of the dragon and from the mouth of the beast, and from the mouth of the false prophet, three foul spirits like frogs,

CHOIR: for they are demonic spirits, performing signs, who go to the kings of the whole world, to assemble them for battle on the great day of God the Almighty.

SON OF MAN: Lo, I am coming like a thief!

GROUP I: Blessed is he who is awake,

GROUP II: Keeping his garments that he may not go naked and be seen exposed.

(*Cut chorus lights, spot on John.*)

JOHN AND CHOIR: And they assembled them at the place which is called in Hebrew (*bright on entire set*) Armageddon! (*Slowly dim.*)

CHOIR: Yea, Lord God the Almighty, true and just are thy judgments!

Scene 7

(*Timpani cadence, dim spot on John. Seventh angel steps forward and pours out bowl as John begins to read.*)

JOHN: The seventh angel poured his bowl into the air . . . and a loud voice came out of the temple, from the throne, saying, . . .

CHOIR: It . . . is . . . done! (*Cut lights, slide 7.*)

JOHN: No one can enter the Temple until it is done! (JOHN *and each of the other readers speak their phrase, then revert to a soft volume level and repeat their phrase over and over, each time with different inflection, tempo, emphasis, etc. to create a constantly changing effect. Readers should come from choir members.*)

(*Stage setting slide out, Scene 1 slide up.*)

READER 2:   . . . foul and evil sores on the people with the mark of the beast!

(*Scene 1 slide out, Scene 2 slide up.*)

READER 3: . . . the sea like the blood of a dead man . . .

(*Scene 2 slide out, Scene 3 slide up.*)

READER 4: . . . rivers and springs of water like blood . . .

(*Scene 3 slide out, Scene 4 slide up.*)

READER 5: . . . searing heat—curses on the name of God . . .

(*Scene 4 slide out, Scene 5 slide up.*)

READER 6: . . . men gnaw their tongues in agony . . . darkness . . .

(*Scene 5 slide out, Scene 6 slide up.*)

READER 7: . . . meeting for war at Armageddon.

(*Scene 6 slide out, Scene 7 slide up.*)

READER 8: It . . . is . . . done! (*All readers stop on word* done.)

JOHN (*spot on* JOHN; *timpani rolls, crescendoing in places of emphasis*): "It is done." Then there came flashes of lightning, rumblings, peals of thunder, and severe earthquake. No earthquake like it has ever occurred since mankind has been on the earth, so tremendous was the quake. The great city split into three parts (*cymbal rolls, brief for effect*) and cities of the nations collapsed. God remembered Babylon the great and gave her the cup filled with the wine of the fury of his wrath. Every island fled away and the mountains could not be found. From the sky, huge hailstones of about a hundred pounds each fell upon people. And they cursed God on account of the plague of hail, because the plague was so terrible. (*All lights off.*)

JOHN: In Act V, I saw the final judgment of God upon Babylon or Rome. In contrast to Act III, Act V brought the complete judgment of God.

Act VI
The Seven Judgments
(Rev. 17:1 to 20:3)

Characters: 2 ANGELS, JOHN, KINGS, MERCHANTS, SAILORS, VOICE FROM THRONE

STAGE SETTING: JOHN, in a pensive mood, is seated on the stage floor in the center of the acting area. The stage is dark with the exception of a soft light focused on JOHN. ANGEL 1 appears to the immediate right of JOHN. A soft light is focused on ANGEL 1 and intensifies as JOHN looks upon the ANGEL; JOHN is startled by the angelic appearance. As the light on the angel intensifies the light on JOHN fades. Music begins as the ANGEL speaks.

Scene 1

ANGEL 1:   John, come I will show you the judgment of the great harlot who is seated upon many waters. She is the mistress of kings and has caused the peoples of the earth to become drunk with the wine of her immorality.

(*The slide of the harlot and beast appears. The angel points to the slide while beckoning* JOHN *to look at it also.* JOHN *rises and does as the angel requests.*)

JOHN: Her name! What does it mean? Babylon the great, mother of harlots and earth's abomination. Who is she? (*Fear and confusion are on his face.*)

(*The slide of the harlot and beast fades out as the angel begins to explain.*)

ANGEL 1:   I will tell you the mystery of the woman and of the beast. The beast that you see was once alive but is now dead. It will rise from the abyss and live again but will eventually be destroyed. The beast is the symbol of Rome's political power and will war with the Lamb, but the Lamb is King of kings and Lord of lords and shall defeat the beast.

(*The slide of an ancient city in its glory appears as the angel continues to explain.*)

ANGEL 1:   The waters surrounding the harlot are peoples from many nations speaking many languages, and the ten horns are ten kings who hate her. These kings will destroy the harlot, the city, leaving her desolate and naked. They will devour her and burn her up with fire. This shall come to pass because God wills it to be and his word shall be fulfilled.

CHOIR (*in a chant*):   Babylon was drunk with the blood of the saints and the blood of the martyrs of Jesus.

(*Music ends. Lights fade. Slide fades.*)

Scene 2

STAGE SETTING: JOHN is standing in the middle of the acting area. A soft light is again focused on him as ANGEL 2 appears to his right. A second soft light focuses upon ANGEL 2 and grows in intensity as the light on

JOHN fades. As the angelic light intensifies JOHN moves toward the angel. A light focuses upon the dancer as music begins. She proceeds to do an interpretive dance of the fall of Babylon. As she begins to dance the angel chants a dirge.)

ANGEL 2:   Fallen, fallen is Babylon the Great! She has become a dwelling place of demons and evil spirits, the haunt of every foul and hateful bird. The nations are drunk with the wine of her impure passion. The kings of the earth have committed fornication with her, and the merchants have grown rich on her sensuality.

(*After the dance is over the music ends and the light on the dancer fades. A light focuses on John. He seems dazed as he turns right to hear an offstage voice. The slide of a burning city depicting a mass exodus appears.*)

CHOIR: Come out of her, my people. Leave her with her sins and plagues— the consequences of God's wrath, or you to shall suffer her fate. Deal with her as she has dealt with you. Repay her twofold. She brags, "I am queen, not a widow. I shall not sorrow, nor grieve." And while she boasts plagues will come; swiftly will come disease, sorrow, famine—destroying her. (*Muted screams and wails from offstage.*) Mighty is the Lord God who passes judgment on her.

(*Final scream from offstage trailing off into silence. Lights fade out quickly. Complete darkness for about ten seconds. The slide of the burning city/mass exodus fades and a slide of the ruins of an ancient city appears. Light focuses upon kings, merchants, sailors.*)

KINGS, MERCHANTS, SAILORS: Alas, Alas! O great city, Babylon!

KINGS: Babylon, you mighty city, your time of judgment has come.

(*Cymbals clash.*)

MERCHANTS: Your fine linen, gold, and jewels are gone. Your wealth is no more.

(*Cymbals clash.*)

SAILORS: Your mighty ships burn upon your waters.

KINGS, MERCHANTS, SAILORS: O Babylon, how swiftly has judgment come upon you!

(*Slide of ruined city fades, light on troupe fades. A light focuses upon ANGEL 2. The ANGEL picks up a millstone and hurls it off the stage, producing the sound of a boulder crashing into water. A second light*) *focuses on* JOHN, *who is standing near the angel.* JOHN *listens as the angel speaks.*)

ANGEL 2:   As this stone was cast into the sea, so shall Babylon be cast away. No more shall music be heard in her streets. The craftsmen and the millers will work no more. What once was light shall soon be dark; life shall be no more. With your witchcraft you have deceived the nations, and you have been found covered with the blood of prophets, saints, and all of those who have been slain on the earth.

(*Lights fade as the scene ends.*)

Scene 3

(*Scene opens in darkness. Illumine third window on left stage.*)

VOICES: Hallelujah! Salvation and glory and power to our God, for his judgments are true and just; he has judged the great harlot who corrupted the earth with her fornication, and he has avenged on her the blood of his servants. Hallelujah! The smoke from her goes up forever and ever.

THE FOUR CREATURES AND THE CHORUS: Hallelujah!

VOICE FROM THE THRONE: Praise our God, all you his servants, you who fear him, small and great.

(*Begin Hallelujah Chorus.*)

CHOIR: Hallelujah! For the Lord our God the Almighty reigns. Let us rejoice and exult and give him the glory; for the marriage of the Lamb has come, and his Bride has made herself ready; it was granted her to be clothed with fine linen, bright and pure.

(*Spotlight on* JOHN *and angel.*)

JOHN: Then an angel appeared and he said to me.

(*John turns to angel.*)

ANGEL: Write this: Blessed are those who are invited to the marriage supper of the Lamb. These are true words of God.

(*Light on table.*)

JOHN: Then I fell at his feet to worship him, but he said to me,

(*As John says this he falls to ground in front of angel. Angel makes him rise and they step to the table.*)

ANGEL: You must not do that! I am a fellow servant with you and your brethren who hold the testimony of Jesus. Worship God.

Scene 4

(*Scene opens in darkness.*)

JOHN: Then I saw heaven open (*spotlights come on* JOHN *with stage lights on low and the picture is illuminated in the fourth window*), and behold a white horse!

NARRATOR: He who sits upon it is called Faithful and True, and in righteousness he judges and makes war.

JOHN: His eyes are like a flame of fire, and on his head are many diadems. He is clad in a robe dipped in blood.

NARRATOR: The name by which he is called is The Word of God.

JOHN: The armies of heaven, arrayed in fine linen, white and pure, followed him on white horses. From his mouth issues a sharp sword with which to smite the nations.

NARRATOR: He will rule them with a rod of iron; he will tread the wine press of the fury of the wrath of God the Almighty.

JOHN: On his robe and on his thigh he has a name inscribed, King of kings and Lord of lords.

(*Scene ends with "The Hallelujah Chorus"—"King of Kings and Lord of Lords." Lights fade to black.*)

Scene 5

(*Scene opens in darkness. Sound of birds—15 seconds. Illuminate* WINDOW 5 *and slide of sun on desert, center stage. White spotlight on* JOHN, *stage right.*)

JOHN: And I saw an angel standing in the sun; and he cried with a loud voice, saying to all the birds that fly in the midst of heaven, . . .

(*Spotlight on* JOHN *fade to black. Slide of birds flying, center stage. Fade up red spotlight on angel—fade in green background lights.*)

ANGEL: Come and gather yourselves together unto the supper of the great God; that you may eat the flesh of kings and the flesh of captains, and the flesh of mighty men, and the flesh of horses, and of them that sit on them, and the flesh of all men, both free and bond, both small and great.

(*Stage goes black as scene ends. Sound of birds—10 seconds.*)

Scene 6

(*Scene opens in darkness. Spotlight opens with* JOHN *standing on the outer edge of the* proskene *to right of stage.*)

JOHN: And I saw the beast and the kings of the earth with their armies gathered to make war against him who sits upon the horse and against his army.

(*Illuminate* WINDOW 6 *on left of stage and slide of horse and rider. Sound of armies.*)

JOHN: And the beast was captured, and with it the false prophet . . . These two were thrown alive into the lake of fire that burns with brimstone.

(*Sounds of screams—slide of fire on center of stage. Lights of all kinds flashing.*)

JOHN: And the rest were slain by the sword of him who sits upon the horse, the sword that issues from his mouth; and all the birds were gorged with their flesh.

(*Flashing lights fade to black. Scene ends.*)

Scene 7

(*Illuminate* WINDOW 7—*very low background lights.*)

JOHN: Then I saw an angel coming down from heaven, holding in his hand the key to the abyss and a great chain. He seized the dragon, the ancient serpent who is the Devil and Satan and bound him for a thousand years . . .

(*Spotlight—angel in cape, kneeling with good-sized, visible key in hand held to floor. As* JOHN *continues,* ANGEL *removes key, pressing other hand —with notable ring—against same spot as if impressing a seal.*)

JOHN (*not pausing*):   And threw him into the abyss and shut it and sealed it over him so that he should deceive the nations no more . . .

(*From this point* ANGEL *stands, pauses, and moves just out of the light to halt with eyes on the "seal."*)

JOHN: Till the thousand years were ended. After that he must be loosed for a little while.

(A seven-count, and fade out lights and window 7.)

JOHN: In Act VI, I saw the fall of Rome and I described it in detail. In a timeless sense, whatever political power arises and is used by evil will in like manner be destroyed. I also saw the end of the age and the return of Christ. He shall conquer evil and Satan.

Act VII
The Seven Great Promises
(Rev. 20:4 to 22:5)

Characters: JOHN, CHOIR, ANGEL, ONE ON THRONE, 4 SAINTS

STAGE SETTING: Stage is dark. Peaceful or joyous music, possibly something from the *Messiah.* Show slide 1 depicting the stage setting in verses 4-5; thrones of the judges before which the souls of the martyrs stand. JOHN begins speaking as the slide is shown and the light slowly comes up to illuminate him. The chorus level remains the same with the throne room of God.

Scene 1

JOHN: Then I saw thrones, and seated on them were those to whom judgment was committed. Also, I saw the souls of those who had been beheaded for their testimony to Jesus and for the word of God, and who had not worshiped the beast or its image and had not received its mark on their foreheads or their hands. They came to life again, and reigned with Christ a thousand years. The rest of the dead did not come to life until the thousand years were ended. This is the first resurrection.

(Lights come up quickly on choir.)

CHOIR: Blessed and holy is he who shares in the first resurrection! Over such the second death has no power, but they shall be priests of God and of Christ, and they shall reign with him a thousand years.

(Slide 1 off. Fade to black all except John. As John speaks, sinister music begins to play. Lights up slowly on SATAN, who is crouched on the floor with hands chained. As JOHN speaks, Satan rises, breaks his chains. Lights up on TWO SAINTS, who worship at cross. Slide 2 [a picture of the earth taken from space] is shown. Satan appears to beckon others.)

JOHN: And when the thousand years are ended, Satan will be loosed from his prison and will come out to deceive the nations which are at the four corners of the earth, that is Gog and Magog, to gather them for battle.

(*Satan crosses to the two saints who cower as Satan circles them and the cross. Sound of tramping feet as martial music is played. Slide 2 off. Slide 3[a photo of fields of Armageddon] and slide 4[a battle scene] are flashed simultaneously. Sounds of battle.*)

JOHN: Their number is like the sand of the sea. And they marched up over the broad earth and surrounded the camp of the saints and the beloved city.

(*Slides 3 and 4 off. Slide 5 [scene of the devil, the beast and the false prophet being cast into the lake of fire] shown. The saints now rise as Satan cowers and backs away from them. Saints seize Satan and cast him into the lake of fire as JOHN speaks.*)

JOHN: But fire came down from heaven and consumed them, and the devil who had deceived them was thrown into the lake of fire and sulphur where the beast and the false prophet were, and they will be tormented day and night for ever and ever.

(*Slide 5 off. Lights fade to black on all except JOHN.*)

Scene 2

(*Lights come up on the One seated on a white throne. Slide 6 [crowd scene] appears on the screen. The One on the throne opens the Book of Life and reads from it. As JOHN speaks, one saint leads Death and Hades to the lake of fire, then leads one of two average people to the lake. The other saint leads the other person to stand beside the One on the throne.*)

JOHN: Then I saw a great white throne and him who sat upon it. And I saw the dead, great and small, standing before the throne, and books were opened. And another book was opened, which is the Book of Life. And the dead were judged by what they had done. And the sea gave up the dead in it, Death and Hades gave up the dead in them, and all were judged by what they had done. Then Death and Hades were thrown into the lake of fire. This is the second death, and if anyone's name was not found written in the Book of Life, he was thrown into the lake of fire.

(*Lights out on all except JOHN. Slide 6 off.*)

Scene 3

(*Slide 7 [scene of the new heaven and the new earth]. Saints and street people stand before the throne. As JOHN speaks, one of the street people kneels before the throne.*)

JOHN: Then I saw a new heaven and a new earth. And I saw the Holy City, new Jerusalem, coming down out of heaven from God, prepared as a bride adorned for her husband.

(Slide 8, new Jerusalem descending is shown.)

ONE ON THRONE: Behold, the dwelling of God is with men. He will dwell with them and they shall be his people, and God himself will be with them; he will wipe away every tear from their eyes, and death shall be no more, neither shall there be mourning nor crying nor pain any more, for the former things have passed away.

(Slides 7 and 8 off. Lights out on all except ONE ON THRONE.)

Scene 4

(Slide 9 [scene of a river, fountain or waterfall, with the Greek letters Alpha and Omega superimposed]. Instrumental version of "Blessed Assurance" plays in the background. Music fades prior to vice list and disappears during list.)

ONE ON THRONE: Behold I make all things new. It is done! I am the Alpha and the Omega, the beginning and the end. To the thirsty I will give from the fountain of the water of life without payment. He who conquers shall have this heritage, and I will be his God and he shall be my son. But as for the cowardly, the faithless, the polluted, as for murderers, fornicators, sorcerers, idolaters, and all liars, their lot shall be in the lake that burns with fire and sulphur, which is the second death.

(Slide 9 off. Lights down to a dark stage.)

Scene 5

(Lights up on JOHN and the angel carrying a bowl and a measuring rod.)

JOHN: Then came one of the seven angels who had the seven bowls full of the seven last plagues.

ANGEL: Come, I will show you the Bride, the wife of the Lamb.

(Slide 10 [scene of the city of the New Jerusalem]. The angel walks JOHN to the side of the slide as four saints, each placed at one corner of the stage, speak; while the saints speak, the angel measures the city.)

JOHN: And in the Spirit he carried me away to a great, high mountain, and he showed me the Holy City of Jerusalem coming down out of heaven from God, having the glory of God. *(The saints speak with enthusiasm and excitement, trying to communicate their joy at having discovered the glory of the city.*)

SAINT 1:   Its radiance is like a most rare jewel,

SAINT 2:   Like a jasper!

SAINT 3:   Clear as crystal!

SAINT 4:   It had a great, high wall, with twelve gates.

SAINT 1:   And on the gates the names of the twelve tribes of the sons of Israel were inscribed.

SAINT 2:   On the east three gates.

SAINT 3:   On the north three gates.

SAINT 4:   On the south three gates.

SAINT 1:   On the west three gates.

SAINT 2:   And the wall of the city had twelve foundations.

SAINT 3:   And on them the twelve names of the twelve apostles of the Lamb.

SAINT 4:   The city lies foursquare.

SAINT 1:   Its length the same as its breadth.

SAINT 2:   It measures twelve thousand stadia!

SAINT 3:   Its length and breadth are equal.

SAINT 4:   Its wall measures a hundred and forty-four cubits by a man's measure!

SAINT 1:   The wall is built of jasper,

SAINT 2:   While the city is pure gold.

SAINT 3:   Clear as glass.

SAINT 4:   The foundations of the wall of the city are adorned with every jewel.

SAINT 1:   The first is jasper.

SAINT 2:   The second sapphire.

SAINT 3:   The third agate.

SAINT 4:   The fourth emerald.

SAINT 1:   The fifth onyx.

SAINT 2:   The sixth carnelian.

SAINT 3:   The seventh chrysolite.

SAINT 4:   The eighth beryl.

SAINT 1:   The ninth topaz.

SAINT 2:   The tenth chrysoprase.

SAINT 3:   The eleventh jacinth.

SAINT 4:   The twelfth amethyst.

SAINT 1:   And the twelve gates were twelve pearls.

SAINT 2:   Each of the gates made of a single pearl!

SAINT 3:   And the street of the city is pure gold.

SAINT 4:   Transparent as glass.

(Lights off on all except JOHN. *Slide 10 remains on screen.)*

Scene 6

(Triumphant, joyous music. JOHN *spotlighted on center stage.)*

JOHN: And I saw no temple in the city, for its temple is the Lord God the
Almighty and the Lamb. And the city has no need of sun or moon to shine
upon it, for the glory of God is its light, and its lamp is the Lamb. By its
light shall the nations walk; and the kings of the earth shall bring their
glory into it, and its gates shall never be shut by day—and there shall be
no night there. But nothing unclean shall enter it, nor any one who
practices abomination or falsehood, but only those who are written in the
Lamb's Book of Life.

(Slide 10 off. JOHN *moves back to left of stage.)*

Scene 7

*(Slide 11 [scene of the river of life] is shown. Peaceful, serene, yet triumphant
music. Lights up on the throne. Around the throne, worshiping, are saints,
angels, and street people.)*

JOHN: Then he showed me the river of the water of life, bright as crystal, flowing from the throne of God and of the Lamb through the middle of the city; also, on either side of the river, the tree of life with its twelve kinds of fruit, yielding its fruit each month; and the leaves of the tree were for the healing of the nations. There shall no more be anything accursed, but the throne of God and of the Lamb shall be in it, and his servants shall worship him; they shall see his face, and his name shall be on their foreheads. And night shall be no more; they need no light of lamp or sun, for the Lord God will be their light, and they shall reign for ever and ever.

(*Slide 11 off. Lights and music slowly fade out.*)

JOHN: In Act VII, I saw scenes which were too beautiful to describe. However, the greatest promise of all was that on the last page of human history I did not see Caesar but the Lamb and God on his throne and they shall rule forever.

Epilogue
(Rev. 22:6-21)

Characters: JOHN, ANGEL, CHOIR, VOICE

STAGE SETTING: (Lights up on the *proskene* and the chorus level. JOHN and the ANGEL are standing in the center of the *proskene,* facing the audience. On the chorus level, several pews have been arranged, so that the chorus members are sitting on the pews, their faces towards JOHN and the angels and their backs toward the audience.)

JOHN (*to audience*):   And the angel said to me,

ANGEL (*to* JOHN):   These words are trustworthy and true. (*to the chorus and audience*) And the Lord, the God of the spirits of the prophets, has sent his angel to show servants what must soon take place.

VOICE: And behold, I am coming soon.

JOHN (*to choir and audience*):   I, John, am he who heard and saw these things.

ANGEL (*to* JOHN):   Do not seal up the words of the prophecy of this book, for the time is near.
    (*to chorus and audience*) Let the evildoer still do evil, and the filthy still be filthy, and the righteous still do right and the holy still be holy.

VOICE: Behold, I am coming soon. . . . I am the Alpha and the Omega, the first and the last, the beginning and the end.

CHOIR: Blessed are those who wash their robes, that they might have the right to the tree of life and that they may enter the city by the gates.

VOICE: I, Jesus, have sent my angel to you with this testimony for the churches. I am the root and the offspring of David, the bright morning star.

JOHN (*to choir and audience, in a persuasive, invitation-type voice*): The Spirit and the Bride say "Come." And let you who hear say "Come." And let you who are thirsty come, let you who desire take the water of life without price. . . . (*Short pause*) He who testifies to these things says,

VOICE: Surely I am coming soon.

JOHN (*loudly and strongly*): Amen. Come Lord Jesus!

(JOHN *drops his arms to his side and bows his head for a pause. Then he lifts his head and lifts his arms over the chorus and audience in a position of benediction.*) "The grace of the Lord Jesus Christ be with all the saints."

CHOIR: (*Sings a seven-fold Amen as the lights fade.*)

Postscript

The following books have been helpful in my study of Revelation and in the writing of *Revelation as Drama*.

BEASLEY-MURRAY, GEORGE. *The Book of Revelation.* Greenwood, South Carolina, The Attic Press, 1974.

BOWMAN, JOHN W. *The First Christian Drama.* Philadelphia: Westminster Press, 1955.

_____. "Revelation, Book of," *The Interpreter's Dictionary of the Bible,* Vol. 4. Nashville: Abingdon Press, 1962.

CAIRD, GEORGE B. *A Commentary on the Revelation of St. John the Divine.* New York: Harper and Row, 1966.

"The Revelation of St. John the Divine," *The Interpreter's Bible,* Vol. XII. Introduction and Exegesis by MARTIN RIST; Exposition by LYNN HAROLD HOUGH. Nashville: Abingdon Press, 1957.

SUMMERS, RAY. *Worthy Is the Lamb.* Nashville: Broadman Press, 1951.

I am grateful to James Freeman and Joe Williamson for their assistance with the early stages of the art included in *Revelation as Drama*.

The model for the theater in Ephesus shown on the back cover is by archaeologist Wilhelm Wilberg. The picture is from W. Alzinger, *Die Spadt def Siebenten Weltwunders,* Vienna Wollzeilen.

J.L.B.